Yes, I Knew!

John H Brennan

Published by John H Brennan, 2023.

While every precaution has been taken in the preparation of this book, the publisher assumes no responsibility for errors or omissions, or for damages resulting from the use of the information contained herein.

YES, I KNEW!

First edition. August 9, 2023.

Copyright © 2023 John H Brennan.

ISBN: 979-8223554851

Written by John H Brennan.

Dedicated to all those Christians searching for a better understanding of how the Blessed Mother Mary played a significant role in Salvation History

Introduction

"Mary, Did You Know?" is a heartwarming and timeless Christmas song that tenderly addresses Mary, the blessed mother of Jesus. Penned by the talented Mark Lowry in 1984, with music composed by the gifted Buddy Greene in 1991, the song has captured the hearts of countless listeners across the world.

The lyrics of this touching hymn beautifully ponder the profound moments of Mary's journey, inviting us to imagine the emotions and thoughts she might have experienced as she carried the divine miracle within her. The lyrics gently inquire whether Mary comprehended the incredible destiny that lay ahead for her and for her child, the very Son of God.

However, it is important to recognize that when Mark Lowry wrote this song, he may have been approaching it from a perspective that reflected his contemporary understanding of the events. At that time, he might not have been fully aware of the cultural and religious context in which Mary lived and how the Jewish people envisioned the liberating Messiah they longed for.

Indeed, Mary's "yes" to God's plan was undoubtedly rooted in her unwavering faith and profound knowledge of the scriptures, which foretold the coming of the Messiah who would bring salvation and freedom to her people. As a devout Jewish young woman, she would have been well-versed in the prophecies that spoke of a Redeemer who would deliver Israel from its bondage.

Throughout what we now call the Old Testament, the anticipation of a Messianic figure was a central theme, promising a powerful and just leader who would restore the nation and usher in an era of peace. Mary, like many Jews of her time, yearned for the fulfillment of these ancient promises. When the angel Gabriel appeared to her, announcing that she would bear the Son of the Most High, she must have recognized the significance of this divine calling and the role her child would play in the grand tapestry of salvation.

As we reflect on Mary's "yes," we must appreciate that it wasn't a decision made in ignorance or uncertainty. Instead, it was a profound act of faith and submission to God's plan, knowing that her child would indeed be the fulfillment of the ages-long hope of her people. With immense courage and devotion, she embraced her role in bringing forth the Savior, who would not only liberate her people from earthly bondage but also offer eternal redemption to all humanity. She knew from her upbringing that both would come at a cost.

"Mary, Did You Know?" remains a cherished Christmas melody, inviting us to share in Mary's wonder and awe as we contemplate the miraculous birth of Jesus Christ. As we listen to its soul-stirring lyrics, we are encouraged to delve deeper into the historical and theological context of Mary's life, recognizing her as a woman of profound faith and understanding, chosen to bear the Light of the world.

Embark on a profound journey of exploration and contemplation as we delve into the soul-stirring question posed by the timeless hymn, "Mary, Did You Know?" Let us traverse the path of the Advent season, where the captivating melodies of Mark and Buddy's creation draw us closer to the essence of Jesus and the profound significance of His life for humanity. In this journey, we shall not only revel in the touching moments when Mary pondered in her heart the miracles unfolding before her eyes, but also uncover the depths of her love for the child she nurtured, the Savior of the world.

As we listen to the enchanting verses of the song during Advent, we are invited to witness the profound mystery of Jesus' incarnation and Mary's pivotal role in this divine plan. We reflect on those precious moments when Jesus, even within the confines of Mary's womb, displayed signs of His divine nature, eliciting tender joy in His mother's heart. Each kick in her womb, a sign of life, foreshadowed the boundless love and sacrifice that this extraordinary child would one day bestow upon humanity.

The manger, a humble feeding trough that cradled the newborn King, serves as a poignant symbol of God's immense humility and love. As we contemplate this miraculous scene, we begin to comprehend the profound meaning behind Jesus' birth in such a lowly setting. Mary, the chosen vessel for this divine incarnation, embraced her role with unwavering faith, fully aware of the tremendous responsibility and sacrifice it entailed.

Through the pages of this compelling book, we journey alongside Mary, witnessing her unyielding devotion to the child she knew was destined for greatness. We come to understand that her "yes" to God's plan was not a momentary decision but an enduring commitment, anchored in her deep understanding of the scriptures and her unwavering trust in God's providence.

As the chapters unfold, we encounter Mary's unwavering support and love for Jesus as He embarked on His earthly ministry. We witness her standing steadfastly at the foot of the cross, enduring immeasurable pain as her beloved son bore the weight of the world's sins. Mary's love transcended the boundaries of motherhood; it encompassed the entire human race, for she understood that Jesus came not only for her but for all of humanity, offering redemption and salvation to those who believed in Him.

In these reflections, we learn that Mary's journey was intertwined with the journey of Jesus, each playing a vital role in God's divine plan of salvation. Her life was marked by unwavering faith, sacrifice, and a profound sense of purpose that continually guided her footsteps.

As we conclude this transformative journey, our love for Mary deepens, and we see her not just as the gentle mother of Jesus but as an exemplar of faith, devotion and trust. Her "yes" echoes through the ages, inspiring us to embrace our own callings with courage and trust, knowing that it all comes at a cost, just as she did.

In the poignant lyrics of "Mary, Did You Know?" and the revelations within these pages, we find a renewed sense of awe and gratitude for the profound love of Jesus and the tender love of Mary. May this journey enrich our Advent experience and draw us closer to the heart of the Christmas story, where love, hope, and redemption intersect in the person of Jesus Christ, the Son of God and Savior of humanity.

The Anticipation Awakens

In the quaint town of Nazareth, young Mary, a curious and thoughtful 10-year-old girl, found herself pondering the prophecies she had heard about the Messiah. One evening, as the sun dipped below the horizon, casting a warm glow over the modest family home, Mary's heart brimmed with questions about the anticipated Savior. She approached her parents, Anne and Joachim, who were sitting by the hearth, the flames flickering and dancing in the dimly lit room.

"Mother, Father," Mary began tentatively, "I've been hearing stories about the Messiah at the synagogue. They say the Messiah will come to save us and bring glory to Israel. But what will it really be like when He comes? What do you think, Father?"

Joachim, a kind and wise man, smiled at his daughter's inquisitive nature. "Ah, my precious Mary," he said, gently ruffling her hair. "The prophecies about the Messiah are indeed profound and varied. Many of our fellow Jews expect the Messiah to be a great political deliverer, much like the valiant King David, who led our people to victory in the past."

Mary's eyes widened with fascination. "So, the Messiah will be a mighty warrior, Father? Will He lead us to triumph over the Romans and free us from their rule?"

Joachim nodded, "Yes, that's what some believe. They hope that the Messiah will bring an end to foreign oppression and restore Israel to its former glory."

"But that's not all," interjected Anne, Mary's gentle and nurturing mother. "According to the prophecies, the Messiah is also foretold to be a descendant of King David, just as God had promised David an eternal dynasty. His lineage will trace back to this great king."

Mary's mind whirled with excitement. "Does that mean the Messiah could come from our family, Mother? Are we descendants of King David?"

Anne smiled warmly, "While we are from the lineage of David, my dear, it's not for us to know exactly who the Messiah will be. We can only wait with hope and faith."

Mary nodded thoughtfully, absorbing the significance of their heritage. "And what else will the Messiah do, Father? Will He be a judge and peacemaker, like the prophets foretold?"

"Indeed," Joachim affirmed. "The Messiah is believed to bring justice and peace to the world, resolving conflicts and ensuring harmony among nations. He will be a righteous judge, guiding us towards a better and more harmonious future."

As Mary continued to listen to her parents' explanations about the Messiah, a thought crossed her mind, and she turned to her father, Joachim, with curiosity shining in her eyes.

"Father," Mary asked hesitantly, "I've been learning about Moses at the synagogue. He was a great leader chosen by God to liberate our ancestors from slavery in Egypt. The stories of how he performed mighty signs and wonders to persuade Pharaoh to let our people go are truly awe-inspiring. Do you think the Messiah will be like Moses too?"

Joachim paused for a moment, appreciating his daughter's keen observation and thoughtful question. He exchanged a knowing glance with Anne before responding, "Your question is perceptive, Mary. The stories of Moses are indeed incredible, and he played a crucial role in our history as a nation. Just like Moses, the Messiah is anticipated to be a liberator, but in a different and even more profound way."

He gently placed his hand on Mary's shoulder, continuing, "You see, my dear, Moses freed our ancestors from physical bondage in Egypt, leading them through the parted waters of the Red Sea to safety.

He showed great signs and wonders, guided by the hand of God. But the Messiah's liberation is of an even deeper kind. He will come to free us not just from earthly oppression but from the chains of sin and separation from God. His signs and wonders will encompass not just the physical realm but also the spiritual, touching our hearts and souls."

Mary nodded, absorbing the profound distinction her father made. "So, the Messiah's liberation is both external and internal, Father?"

"Yes, exactly," Joachim confirmed with a gentle smile. "The Messiah will offer us true freedom, a freedom that brings wholeness and reconciliation with God. He will show us the path to eternal life and salvation."

Mary's mind raced with thoughts as she began to grasp the profound nature of the Messiah's mission. "And like Moses, will the Messiah lead us to a promised land, a place of prosperity and spiritual renewal?"

Anne chimed in, "In a way, my dear, yes. The Messiah's mission is not only about leading us to a physical land but to a state of spiritual abundance and unity with God. He will guide us towards righteousness and a deeper understanding of our faith, ultimately leading us to the heavenly kingdom."

"I see," Mary replied thoughtfully, her heart stirred by the significance of the Messiah's mission. "The Messiah will liberate us in ways we cannot even fully comprehend yet, just as Moses did for our ancestors."

Joachim nodded in agreement. "Indeed, Mary. The anticipation of the Messiah's coming fills us with hope and excitement, as we know that His arrival will bring immeasurable blessings and a fulfillment of God's promises."

As the family continued their conversation, Mary's young heart was filled with a renewed sense of wonder and reverence for the Messiah. She felt a growing anticipation for the day when this long-awaited Savior would come, bringing liberation and redemption to all humanity. And in her innocence and faith, she knew that her people's story would forever be intertwined with the profound and miraculous chapter yet to unfold—the coming of the Messiah.

As Mary's parents spoke, her imagination soared. "Will the Messiah also be a spiritual teacher, Mother?" she inquired.

Anne's eyes sparkled with pride at her daughter's keen insights. "Yes, Mary, that is also a part of the Messiah's role. He will be a teacher of divine wisdom, guiding people in understanding God's laws and principles. He will lead us on a path of righteousness and spiritual renewal."

Mary absorbed all this information with a sense of wonder. "And will the Messiah rebuild or restore the Temple in Jerusalem, Father? The synagogue elders mentioned that as well."

Joachim nodded gravely. "Yes, that's a belief held by some. The Temple holds immense religious significance for our people, and its restoration or rebuilding is sometimes connected to the messianic expectations. It represents a symbol of spiritual connection and renewal for the entire nation."

As the evening wore on, Mary's heart overflowed with gratitude for the insightful conversation with her parents. She had gained a deeper understanding of the varied and profound beliefs surrounding the Messiah. The anticipation and hope for the coming of the Savior were palpable, and Mary realized that each element of the messianic figure held a unique promise of salvation and restoration.

In the days that followed, Mary continued to contemplate the prophecies, nurturing her faith in the promise of a Messiah who would bring hope, liberation, and spiritual renewal to her people. She knew one day the Savior would enter the world, bringing love, redemption, and peace to all humanity. She, with a young girl's heart beating with anticipation, wondered if her humble town of Nazareth, would produce the Messiah who would play a pivotal role in the grand tapestry of God's divine plan.

Laws and Breaking the Laws

As a devout Jewish girl, Mary grew up with a strong understanding of the importance of following the laws of God as prescribed in the Torah, which includes the commandments and regulations given to the Israelites in the Hebrew Bible.

The Jewish faith places a central emphasis on obedience to God's commandments and living a righteous life in accordance with His teachings. Young Mary grew up surrounded by the teachings of the ancient scriptures and the profound significance of observing God's commandments. From a tender age, her parents instilled in her a deep reverence for the covenant relationship between God and the people of Israel.

One evening a couple days later, as the sun began to set, Mary found herself sitting with her mother, Anne, by the open window, bathed in the gentle glow of twilight. The scent of fresh bread wafted from the kitchen, and the soft murmurs of prayer could be heard from the synagogue nearby. The atmosphere was serene, perfect for a heartfelt conversation.

"Mother," Mary began with a touch of solemnity, "I have been thinking about the covenant God made with our ancestors. The stories we have learned at the synagogue speak of blessings for obedience and discipline for disobedience. What really happens if we don't follow God's commandments?"

Anne smiled tenderly, her wise gaze resting on her daughter. "Ah, my dear Mary, understanding the implications of not following God's commandments is an essential aspect of our faith. You are right; God established a covenant with our people, promising blessings and protection when we remain obedient to His laws. However, there are also consequences when we stray from His ways."

Mary nodded thoughtfully, recalling the stories she had learned from the scriptures. "Like when our ancestors wandered in the desert for forty years because they did not trust in God's guidance," she added.

"Exactly," Anne replied, her voice gentle but firm. "Their lack of faith and obedience led to a time of discipline and wandering until they learned to fully rely on God. The stories of our history hold valuable lessons, reminding us of the importance of staying faithful to the covenant. God really wants us to love Him, as He loves us. But God knows the evil one tempted Adam and Eve. Although God talked to them every day and gave them everything they wanted, the evil one convinced them that God was a jealous God, not wanting to share with them the gift of knowledge"

Mary was confused, saying "I go to Hebrew school and you and father teach me all I could ever want to learn. What more knowledge is there to learn?" Anne smiled and said "Yes, Mary, you are right. The evil one can make anyone insecure, even when the truth is shared. The fear of being left out of something can make even those with strong faith break His covenant."

Mary's brow furrowed in thought. "But what kind of consequences might we face today if we don't follow God's commandments?"

Anne took a moment to gather her thoughts, recognizing the weight of the question in her daughter's eyes. "The consequences may vary, my dear," she explained. "When we stray from God's ways, we risk distancing ourselves from His blessings and guidance. Disobedience may lead to feelings of emptiness, discontent, or even hardships in life. It is not that God desires to punish us, but rather, He wants us to live in harmony with His divine plan for our lives."

Mary absorbed her mother's words, realizing the importance of aligning her actions with God's will. "So, by following His commandments, we open ourselves to His blessings and protection?"

Anne nodded, a tender smile gracing her lips. "Yes, my child. When we live in obedience to God's laws, we invite His love and guidance into our lives. It is a path of righteousness and a deepening of our covenant relationship with Him."

As the conversation continued, Mary's understanding of the covenant relationship deepened. She realized that God's commandments were not just a set of rules to follow, but a pathway to a life filled with purpose, meaning, and divine blessings. She understood that following the covenant was more about growing in love with God who loved us rather than rules we will be punished for if we slip up.

Her young heart embraced the wisdom her mother shared, and she resolved to honor the covenant by faithfully observing God's commandments throughout her life. And in this sacred exchange of knowledge and love, the bond between Mary and her mother grew stronger, nurturing a legacy of faith that would forever shape the course of history.

The next morning, the sun gently peeked over the horizon, casting a warm glow on Mary's room as she and her mother, Anne, sat together at the small wooden table. The aroma of fresh bread and warm herbal tea filled the air, and the tranquility of the morning enveloped them like a comforting embrace.

"Mother," Mary began, her voice tinged with curiosity, "yesterday, we talked about the covenant and the consequences of not following God's commandments. But what if someone does sin and disobeys those laws? What happens then?"

Anne looked at her daughter with a tender expression, recognizing the sincerity in her question. "My dear Mary, sin is indeed a part of our human nature. It is the act of disobeying God's laws and moral principles outlined in the Torah. When one commits a sin, it creates a separation between that person and God, and it can also have negative consequences for the individual and the community."

Mary listened attentively, her heart yearning to understand the deeper implications of sin and its effect on one's relationship with God.

Anne continued, "However, our faith teaches us about the opportunity for repentance, or teshuvah, which is a profound act of turning back to God. When a person realizes their wrongdoing and feels sincere remorse, they can seek forgiveness through confession and a genuine commitment to change their ways."

"Repentance sounds like a chance for reconciliation," Mary mused, her young mind absorbing the significance of teshuvah.

Anne nodded, her eyes shining with wisdom. "Indeed, my child. Repentance is a path to forgiveness and reconciliation with God. It allows us to mend our relationship with Him and seek His guidance once more. Our tradition teaches us that God is compassionate and merciful, and when we sincerely repent, He forgives us."

Mary's heart swelled with hope at the thought of God's forgiveness. "But how does one truly repent, Mother? What does it involve?"

Anne smiled, touched by her daughter's earnestness. "Repentance is a multi-faceted process. It begins with recognizing our wrongdoing and feeling genuine remorse for our actions. We must confess our sins to God, seeking His forgiveness with a contrite heart. It also requires a sincere effort to change our ways and strive to do better in the future."

"And when we take these steps," Mary asked, "God forgives us?"

"Yes, my dear," Anne replied with assurance. "When we approach God with a humble heart and make a sincere effort to change, He extends His forgiveness and opens the door to reconciliation. Repentance is an essential part of our faith, offering us a chance to grow and draw closer to God."

As the discussion between Mary and her mother, Anne, continued, they delved deeper into the concept of making amends after breaking a covenant with God. Mary listened intently, eager to understand the significance of repairing the bond with God when they faltered in obedience.

"Mother," Mary inquired with a thoughtful expression, "when we break a covenant with God, what can we do to show Him that we are truly remorseful for our actions?"

Anne smiled gently at her daughter's genuine curiosity, appreciating her desire to grasp the depth of their faith. "My dear, when we find ourselves in the regrettable situation of breaking a covenant with God, there are steps we can take to seek reconciliation with Him."

She continued, "First, we need to acknowledge our wrongdoing, taking responsibility for our actions without making excuses. Then, we must apologize sincerely to God, expressing genuine remorse for disappointing Him."

Mary nodded, understanding the importance of genuine remorse. "And what else can we do, Mother?"

Anne explained, "Sometimes, to symbolize our sincerity, we may offer a sign of our remorse. We would present offerings at the Temple as a way to seek forgiveness. These offerings, like turtle doves, lambs, or other animals, were a visible way to demonstrate their commitment to making amends."

Mary's eyes widened with curiosity. "So, by offering an animal, they showed God that they were truly sorry and wanted to mend the covenant?"

"Yes, my dear," Anne affirmed. "It is a tangible way to communicate their desire to repair the relationship with God. These offerings represented a willingness to make restitution and reaffirm their commitment to follow God's commandments."

Mary pondered for a moment before asking another question, "And if we offend God's covenant today, do we still offer animal sacrifices?"

Anne gently shook her head. "Yes, my dear, we offer animal sacrifices just as our ancestors did. We also seek reconciliation through heartfelt prayers, seeking God's forgiveness and grace. We can still show our sincerity by making efforts to change our ways, to walk in righteousness, and to be obedient to God's teachings."

As they continued their conversation, Mary gained a deeper appreciation for the significance of making amends with God. She realized that seeking reconciliation required more than just words; it involved genuine actions to show remorse and a renewed commitment to follow the path of righteousness. The concept of repentance and making amends brought forth a sense of responsibility and reverence in her heart, inspiring her to be mindful of her actions and choices in her relationship with God.

As the morning sun bathed them in its gentle light, Mary felt a profound sense of peace and understanding. She realized that while sin was an inevitable aspect of human life, the path of repentance provided an opportunity for healing and renewal. The love and compassion of God enveloped her heart, reassuring her that no matter the mistakes she might make along her journey, the way of teshuvah would always be open to her.

In this tender exchange of knowledge and faith, the bond between Mary and her mother deepened, strengthening the legacy of wisdom that would guide Mary's steps on the path of righteousness and bring her even closer to the heart of God. And as they embraced the new day, the warmth of their shared faith filled their souls, creating a sacred space where love, forgiveness, and reconciliation with the Divine awaited them, offering hope and grace to all who sought to return to God's embrace through repentance.

Girl Talk

Mary was just finishing her morning chores and was eager to spend the day playing with her friends, Hannah and Rachel. Just as she stepped out of her house, she saw Hannah and Rachel approaching with big smiles on their faces.

"Mary, can you come out to play with us?" Hannah asked eagerly.

"Of course! I just finished my chores," Mary replied with a joyful grin as she turned to tell her mom where she was going.

The three friends skipped down the path, giggling and chatting as they made their way to a nearby field. They jumped rope, played tag, and chased butterflies, thoroughly enjoying their carefree time together.

As they caught their breath under the shade of a tree, Hannah shared her exciting news. "Guess what, guys? My family and I just came back from Jerusalem. We visited the Temple, and I saw something so strange and solemn."

Curiosity sparked in Mary's eyes. "What did you see, Hannah?"

Hannah's voice took on a serious tone as she recounted her experience. "At the Temple, I saw the priests performing a special ritual with an animal. They said it was a sacrifice for the repentance of sin."

Mary kind of knew where this might lead, as she and her parents had just talked about it. "Repentance of sin? What does that mean?" Rachel asked, her curiosity piqued.

Hannah explained, "Well, they said that when someone does something really wrong, they have to show they are sorry to God. And one way to do that is to offer an animal as a sign of their repentance.

The animal's life is taken as a way to symbolize the seriousness of sin and the need to turn back to God."

Rachel inquisitively furrowed her brow, trying to comprehend the solemnity of the ritual. "But why an animal? Why does an innocent life have to be taken for the sins of another?"

Hannah nodded, understanding her friend's confusion. "I think it's because an animal's life is precious, and it reminds us of the consequences of our actions. It shows that sin has serious consequences, and we must strive to live righteously and seek forgiveness."

Rachel chimed in, "So, by offering an animal, they are saying sorry to God, and it's like a promise to do better?"

"Yes, exactly," Hannah affirmed. "It's a way to demonstrate sincere remorse and the desire to change for the better. The offering is a visible symbol of repentance, reminding us of the need to be mindful of our actions and strive to be righteous."

"I wonder if we would ever have to offer a sacrifice," Rachel pondered, swinging on a nearby swing.

Mary shook her head, her heart heavy with the thought. "I hope not, but it's essential to remember that we should try our best to follow God's commandments and be kind and loving to others. That way, we can avoid causing harm and having to make such sacrifices."

Hannah added, "Yes, and even if we do make mistakes, we can always seek forgiveness through prayer and teshuvah—repentance. God is loving and forgiving, and when we truly regret our actions and try to do better, we can mend our relationship with Him."

As the girls talked, they began to see the significance of the sacrifices in a new light. It wasn't just about the act of offering an animal, but rather about the deeper understanding of sin and the importance of striving to be righteous in their actions and choices.

"We should always remember the lessons we learn from the rituals at the Temple," Mary said thoughtfully. "It's a reminder that our actions have consequences, and we should strive to do what's right and good.

It's always better to truly love God with your whole heart and soul than to live in fear of upsetting your relationship with him."

Hannah and Rachel nodded in agreement. Their playful afternoon had turned into a moment of reflection and understanding, deepening their appreciation for their faith and the importance of living a life aligned with God's teachings.

As the girls made their way back home, the conversation lingered in their hearts. They knew that their friendship was not only about laughter and fun but also about supporting each other in their journey of faith and understanding. And in the quiet moments of the evening, the echoes of their shared wisdom would continue to shape their young hearts, nurturing a profound reverence for God's teachings and the path of righteousness they were determined to follow. The lessons from their day of play would stay with them, guiding their actions and choices as they grew in their faith and friendship.

God's Promises and Warnings

As the sun began to set, casting a warm orange glow over the landscape, Mary made her way back home after a day filled with laughter and play with her friends, Hannah and Rachel. Their joyful memories lingered in her heart as she approached her humble dwelling, excited to share her day's adventures with her parents, Anne and Joachim.

Upon entering the house, Mary found her parents sitting by the flickering light of an oil lamp. They looked up with loving smiles as Mary joined them, her eyes shining with excitement.

"Mother, Father, you won't believe the day I had with Hannah and Rachel!" Mary exclaimed, settling down beside them.

Her parents chuckled, eager to hear all about her day. "Tell us everything, dear," Anne said.

But before Mary could launch into her tales, Joachim gently interrupted, "Let us first pray the evening prayers together, thanking God for the blessings of this day and seeking His guidance for the night ahead."

Mary nodded, and the family joined hands in prayer. They bowed their heads, offering words of gratitude and praise to God for His goodness and protection. They sought His wisdom and guidance, asking for blessings upon their family and friends.

After the prayer, they released each other's hands and looked at one another with serene expressions. "Now, my dear," Anne said, "as we eat our evening meal, you can share with us the events of your day."

Mary launched into a lively account of their day's activities - the games they played, the butterflies they chased, and the tales they shared. But as the conversation flowed, Hannah's mention of the Temple and sacrificial offerings lingered in her mind.

"We had such fun, but we also talked about something serious today," Mary began thoughtfully. "Hannah told us about seeing the priests at the Temple performing sacrifices for repentance of sins."

Anne and Joachim exchanged a knowing glance. They were well aware of the significance of sacrifices in their faith and the teachings that surrounded them. They had hoped that their discussions the previous days with Mary had satisfied her curiosity about the consequences of sin.

"Yes, my dear," Joachim responded gently. "Sacrifices and offerings have been an essential part of our people's worship and relationship with God."

Mary's curiosity grew as she listened to her parents explain further.

"God has given us promises and warnings in His teachings," Anne continued. "When we follow His laws and live righteously, He promises blessings and protection for the faithful. He is a loving and providing God, as we read in Leviticus - "

If you follow my decrees and are careful to obey my commands, I will send you rain in its season, and the ground will yield its crops and the trees their fruit. Your threshing will continue until grape harvest and the grape harvest will continue until planting, and you will eat all the food you want and live in safety in your land.

I will grant peace in the land, and you will lie down and no one will make you afraid. I will remove wild beasts from the land, and the sword will not pass through your country. You will pursue your enemies, and they will fall by the sword before you. Five of you will chase a hundred, and a hundred of you will chase ten thousand, and your enemies will fall by the sword before you.

I will look on you with favor and make you fruitful and increase your numbers, and I will keep my covenant with you. You will still be eating last year's harvest when you will have to move it out to make room for the new. I will put my dwelling place among you, and I will not abhor you. I will walk among you and be your God, and you will be my people. I am the Lord your God, who brought you out of Egypt so that you would no longer be slaves to the Egyptians; I broke the bars of your yoke and enabled you to walk with heads held high.

Joachim added, "But it's also important to heed the warnings of judgment for disobedience. In Deuteronomy, we see the consequences of straying from God's path, such as exile and dispersion among the nations."

Then the Lord will scatter you among all nations, from one end of the earth to the other. There you will worship other gods—gods of wood and stone, which neither you nor your ancestors have known. Among those nations you will find no repose, no resting place for the sole of your foot. There the Lord will give you an anxious mind, eyes weary with longing, and a despairing heart. You will live in constant suspense, filled with dread both night and day, never sure of your life. In the morning you will say, "If only it were evening!" and in the evening, "If only it were morning!"—because of the terror that will fill your hearts and the sights that your eyes will see. The Lord will send you back in ships to Egypt on a journey I said you should never make again. There you will offer yourselves for sale to your enemies as male and female slaves, but no one will buy you.

Mary's eyes widened with understanding. "So, God's promises and warnings serve as incentives for obedience and reminders of the consequences of our actions?"

"Exactly, my dear," Anne nodded. "They guide us to make righteous choices and stay on the path of goodness. We don't mean to scare you, but God is not only a loving God, but also a jealous and vengeful God."

Mary then asked about sacrifices and atonement, eager to learn more about the rituals that Hannah had witnessed.

"Sacrifices have always been an integral part of ancient Jewish practice," Joachim explained. "They were meant to seek forgiveness and atonement for sins. Different offerings, like sin offerings and guilt offerings, were prescribed in the Torah to demonstrate repentance and seek God's forgiveness."

"But why did they offer animals?" Mary inquired, remembering Hannah's explanation.

"Offering an animal was a way to symbolize the seriousness of sin," Anne replied. "It reminded the people of the consequences of their actions and the need for reconciliation with God. Sacrifices were visible expressions of repentance and seeking forgiveness. This is why the animal has to be without blemish – a good strong animal that it is hard to part with."

Joachim said, "Mary, I am sure you've heard this several times at Temple, but let's talk about it here. The sacrificial system is well detailed in the Torah, specifically in the books of Leviticus and Deuteronomy. There are several types of offerings, each serving a specific purpose and symbolizing different aspects of devotion and atonement. Some of the common types of offerings included burnt offerings, grain offerings, peace offerings, sin offerings, and guilt offerings."

Mary's father continued, "The process of offering sacrifices involved specific rituals and procedures that are meticulously followed. Here's how it generally works. First, the appropriate sacrifice is chosen. The type of offering depends on the purpose of the offering and the individual's circumstances. For example, a burnt offering was an expression of complete surrender to God, while a sin offering was made to seek forgiveness for unintentional sins. People would travel to Jerusalem, especially during major festivals and significant occasions and while there, they offer their sacrifices at the Temple. Once they arrived at the Temple, there were designated areas for offering the sacrifices. People form lines, waiting their turn to present their offerings to the priests."

He continued, "The priests, serve as intermediaries between the people and God. They would inspect the animals or items being offered to ensure they met the requirements outlined in the Torah. The offerings were to be without blemish and of the specified age and gender, again fully prescribed in the scriptures. Once the offering was approved, the person making the sacrifice would participate in the ritual under the guidance of the priests. Specific prayers and incense would be used during the process, signifying the act of devotion and consecration."

"In the case of burnt offerings, the entire animal would be consumed by fire on the altar. For other types of offerings, the priests would keep certain portions for themselves, while the remainder of the meat would often be returned to the person offering the sacrifice. Some offerings are made on a daily basis, while others were reserved for specific occasions and festivals. For instance, the burnt offering is offered every morning and evening as a continual act of devotion."

Mary nodded, taking in the wisdom shared by her parents. She felt a profound sense of gratitude for their guidance and for the teachings that illuminated their faith. The stories from their sacred scriptures now held deeper meaning, guiding her to make choices aligned with God's will and reminding her of the path of righteousness.

As the evening settled around them, the lamp's gentle glow casting a warm ambiance, Mary felt a sense of contentment. The conversations with her parents had deepened her understanding of God's promises, warnings, and the significance of sacrifices. She knew that her journey of faith and learning had just begun, and she felt blessed to have her parents as her guides, leading her closer to God's love and wisdom. And in the embrace of her family's love, she found solace, knowing that their shared faith would be the foundation of their bond, guiding them through life's joys and challenges with a profound trust in God's providence.

Social Responsibility

As the morning sun gently illuminated Mary's room, she woke up feeling a sense of renewed curiosity about the impact of not following the laws God had given their people. The previous day's conversation with her friends, Hannah and Rachel, about sacrificial offerings and God's promises and warnings lingered in her thoughts. She knew there was much more to explore and understand.

After eating some fresh figs, bread, and sipping on fruit juice, Mary joined her mother, Anne, in their small prayer space. They bowed their heads together, offering their morning prayers of gratitude and seeking God's guidance for the day ahead. As they finished, Mary took a deep breath, feeling a newfound eagerness to explore another aspect of their faith.

"Mother, I have something on my mind," Mary began hesitantly. "Yesterday, while playing with Hannah and Rachel, we talked about sacrifices and God's promises and warnings. But I also learned about our responsibility as a community to care for one another."

Anne smiled gently, seeing the spark of curiosity in her daughter's eyes. "Yes, my dear, that is an important aspect of our faith - community and social responsibility. We have commandments that promote social justice and compassion, guiding us to care for the less fortunate and treat others with kindness."

Mary nodded, her interest growing. "Like giving to the poor, protecting the widow and orphan, and treating strangers with kindness?"

"Yes, exactly," Anne affirmed. "In Deuteronomy, we are told to open our hand to the poor and needy, and in Exodus, we are commanded to protect those who have lost their husbands or parents. Furthermore, Leviticus reminds us to treat strangers with kindness, as we were once strangers in the land of Egypt."

"But what happens if we don't show love and compassion to others in our community?" Mary asked, her curiosity leading her deeper into understanding the consequences.

Anne's expression softened as she gently explained, "When we neglect our responsibility to care for one another, there can be repercussions. Our actions, or lack thereof, have an impact on the harmony of our community. If we fail to show love and compassion to those in need, it can lead to division and strife, creating a society that lacks justice and empathy."

Mary absorbed her mother's words, her heart filled with a sense of responsibility. She understood that their faith called for not only personal righteousness but also a commitment to building a just and caring society where everyone's needs were considered.

"I want to learn more about this, Mother," Mary said earnestly. "I want to understand how we can be better community members and live in harmony with others, just as God intended."

Anne embraced her daughter warmly, proud of her growing understanding and desire to explore the depths of their faith. "Of course, my dear. I'm here to guide you every step of the way. Together, we'll delve into the teachings that foster a loving and just community, and we'll strive to live by these principles, spreading kindness and compassion wherever we go. Always remember to love God with your entire heart and soul and also, love one another as God loves you. If we can all do that, this will be a happy place to live until we are rewarded in our eternal life"

With a renewed sense of purpose, Mary knew that her journey of faith had taken a meaningful turn. She was determined to embrace the teachings of community and social responsibility, carrying them in her heart as she navigated life's path. And as she continued to learn and grow, she knew that her faith would not only enrich her life but also inspire her to be a beacon of love and compassion for others, creating a ripple of positive change in their community and beyond.

In the days that followed, Mary immersed herself in the teachings of community and social responsibility. With her mother's guidance, she delved into the sacred scriptures, exploring the commandments that emphasized caring for the less fortunate and treating others with kindness and compassion.

As she read passages like Deuteronomy, Exodus, and Leviticus, Mary's heart swelled with a deep sense of empathy. She understood that being part of a community meant not only following God's laws for personal righteousness but also actively reaching out to help others and uplift those in need.

In Deuteronomy, Mary learned that God commands His people to be open-handed and generous towards the poor and needy among them. He encourages them to freely give to those who are in need, without hesitation or reluctance, as an act of compassion and kindness.

In the Exodus verses, Mary is reminded that God emphasizes the importance of protecting the vulnerable members of society, such as widows and orphans. He warns against mistreating them and assures that if they cry out to Him in their distress, He will hear their cries and respond with judgment upon those who have wronged them.

In Leviticus, God instructs His people to treat strangers with kindness and fairness. He reminds them that they were once strangers in the land of Egypt, and thus, they should have empathy and compassion towards foreigners residing among them. They are called to love them as they love themselves, acknowledging that they, too, were once outsiders in a foreign land.

Mary took every opportunity to put these teachings into practice. When she saw someone in the village struggling, whether it was a widow who had lost her husband or a family in need of assistance, she lent a helping hand. She and her friends, Hannah and Rachel, started collecting extra bread and fruits from their families to share with those who had little.

Their small acts of kindness soon began to spread throughout the village. The neighbors noticed the girls' compassion and were inspired to join them in supporting the less fortunate. The sense of community grew stronger, and a spirit of mutual care and support flourished among the villagers.

One evening, as the village gathered for a communal meal, Mary saw firsthand the positive impact their actions had on their community. The smiles on the faces of the families they had helped and the sense of togetherness filled her heart with joy. The village had become more than just a collection of houses; it was a place where everyone looked out for one another.

As time passed, Mary's understanding of community and social responsibility deepened. She realized that by living in harmony with others and showing kindness, they were not only following God's commandments but also creating a society that reflected His love and compassion.

One day, as Mary and her mother were sitting in their prayer space, Mary couldn't help but express her gratitude for the lessons she had learned.

"Mother, I'm so thankful for all you've taught me about community and social responsibility," Mary said with a warm smile. "It's made me see the true essence of our faith - that it's not just about individual piety, but about creating a loving and caring community."

Anne beamed with pride at her daughter's insight. "You have grown into a wise and compassionate young woman, Mary. I'm so proud of the person you are becoming."

The bond between mother and daughter deepened as they shared their faith, supporting and inspiring one another to live in accordance with God's teachings. Mary knew that her journey of faith was a lifelong endeavor, and she was grateful to have her mother as her constant guide and companion.

As Mary continued to live out these principles, her actions touched the lives of many. Her kindness and compassion became a source of inspiration for others, and soon, their village became known for its strong sense of unity and care for one another.

And so, Mary's journey continued, fueled by her unwavering faith, love for her community, and her commitment to making a positive impact on the lives of others. With each passing day, she knew that she was not only following God's commandments but also living out the essence of her faith - to love one another and be a shining example of compassion and kindness for all to see.

Day of Atonement

Yom Kippur, approached with an air of reverence and anticipation in the village where Mary lived with her parents, Anne and Joachim. As the holiest day in the Jewish calendar, Yom Kippur was a time of introspection, repentance, and seeking forgiveness for sins committed throughout the year. For Mary and her family, it was a day deeply ingrained with tradition and faith.

In the days leading up to Yom Kippur, the entire village prepared for the sacred occasion. Homes were meticulously cleaned, and the aroma of freshly baked challah, a special braided bread with flour, eggs, oil and honey filled the air. Mary and her mother spent time together in the kitchen, carefully preparing traditional dishes to share with family and neighbors after the fast.

As the sun set on the evening before Yom Kippur, Mary joined her parents and the rest of the village at the synagogue for the Kol Nidre service, where the haunting melody of the ancient prayer filled the sacred space. In the dimly lit sanctuary, the community came together as one, seeking forgiveness and renewal of their spirits.

The next morning, the village awoke to a hushed stillness. Yom Kippur had arrived. It was a day of fasting, reflection, and prayer. Mary and her parents dressed in their finest white garments, symbolizing purity and spiritual cleansing. They walked hand in hand to the local temple, where a solemn atmosphere enveloped them.

During the Yom Kippur service, the words of the prayers resonated deeply within Mary's heart. She thought of the conversations she had with her friends, Hannah and Rachel, about sacrificial offerings and the significance of repentance. The concept of seeking forgiveness through offerings seemed to intertwine with the essence of Yom Kippur, a day dedicated to atonement and reconciliation.

As the service progressed, Mary observed her parents bowing their heads in prayer with a sense of humility and devotion. Anne's eyes were closed, her lips moving silently in conversation with God. Joachim's hands trembled slightly as he held the prayer book, his heart pouring out sincere petitions for forgiveness.

After the morning service, Mary and her parents returned home. The day was filled with periods of deep reflection, prayer, and reading from the scriptures. As the sun reached its pinnacle, the village gathered once again at the synagogue for the most solemn part of Yom Kippur - the recitation of the Vidui, the confession of sins.

In a hushed voice, the congregation recited a long list of sins, acknowledging their human imperfections and seeking God's mercy. The sins professed, were read together but as if each person professing had committed each and every sin. As a community, they may have committed each sin, and because their lives within the community were intertwined, each should seek atonement for each sin. Mary felt a profound sense of vulnerability, as if the weight of her own shortcomings had become palpable.

During the public confession, as the transgressions are listed, worshipers humbly place their hands over their hearts, acknowledging the weight of each mistake. This solemn act symbolizes the responsibility our hearts bear in leading us astray, sometimes into sins of greed, lust, and anger. It serves as a heartfelt reminder of our human fallibility and the need for sincere repentance to seek forgiveness and grow spiritually.

During these prayers, Mary recalled her conversations with Hannah and Rachel about the sacrificial offerings. She realized that the offerings - the act of sincere repentance and seeking forgiveness - was still deeply ingrained in the Yom Kippur rituals.

As the afternoon wound down, many of the villagers from Nazareth able to travel down to the Jordan River about 10 miles away, while others went to small streams and ponds nearby. Once gathered at the banks of the river, in a beautiful tradition, each person cast away a symbolic stone into the water, representing the casting away of their sins and the hope for a clean slate.

On the way back up the hill to their home in Nazareth with her parents, a profound sense of gratitude filled Mary's heart. She felt humbled by the opportunity to seek forgiveness and embark on a new beginning. The sacrificial offerings of the past may have been physical, but Mary understood that the true essence of atonement and seeking God's grace was an offering of the heart - a genuine desire to be better and draw closer to God.

As they struggled the lofty hill in front of them, Mary pondered the what it really would mean to fulfill the atonement of the confession prayers of the Vidui. How could anyone really take on the sins of the entire community and atone for them all?

As the stars began to twinkle in the darkening sky, the villagers once again gathered at the synagogue. The haunting melody of the Ne'ilah service filled the air, signaling the closing of the gates of heaven. It was a moment of deep intensity, as the community offered its final prayers and entreaties to God before the day came to a close.

In the embrace of her parents, Mary experienced a profound sense of peace. Yom Kippur had been a day of soul-searching, of acknowledging faults, and of seeking God's forgiveness and guidance. The lessons of the sacrificial offerings intertwined with the spirit of the holy day, reinforcing the importance of sincere repentance and living in accordance with God's laws.

As the Yom Kippur fast came to an end, the village erupted into joyous celebrations. Families came together, breaking the fast with traditional dishes, including honey cakes and sweet pastries, symbolizing hopes for a sweet and fruitful year ahead.

In the midst of the celebrations, Mary found herself surrounded by her friends, Hannah and Rachel. Together, they shared stories of their Yom Kippur experiences and the insights they had gained. They spoke of the significance of seeking forgiveness, the power of sincere repentance, and the reminder that God's love and mercy were boundless.

For Mary, Yom Kippur had become more than just a day of rituals and prayers. It had become a profound journey of the heart, a time of self-discovery, and a testament to the enduring spirit of their faith. As she looked around at the faces of her family and friends, she felt a deep sense of gratitude for the bonds of community, for the teachings that guided their lives, and for the assurance that God's providence and deliverance were steadfast.

As Mary lay in bed after the long day of Yom Kippur, her heart was filled with a profound sense of peace and reflection. The echoes of the day's prayers, the solemn Viddui, and the symbolic act of casting away sins at the riverbank lingered in her mind.

As she thought about the significance of Yom Kippur and the teachings she had learned from her parents and the community, she couldn't help but recall the lessons about the prophets. The words of Isaiah, Jeremiah, and other messengers of God resonated within her soul.

The prophetic messages had taught her about the call for justice, compassion, and righteousness. They had warned of the consequences of disobedience and the importance of living in alignment with God's will. She understood that seeking forgiveness and repentance were not merely rituals but a heartfelt commitment to lead a life of virtue and love.

In the quiet stillness of her room, Mary felt a renewed sense of purpose. She knew that Yom Kippur was not just a once-a-year event but a constant reminder of the need for self-examination, humility, and the determination to live with integrity.

With the words of the prophets guiding her thoughts, Mary made a heartfelt prayer. She prayed for strength to follow God's path, for compassion to care for those in need, and for wisdom to discern right from wrong.

As she drifted off to sleep, Mary felt a deep sense of gratitude. Yom Kippur had been a day of soul-searching and spiritual growth, a day that had rekindled her commitment to embrace the prophetic messages of justice, compassion, and righteousness.

With each passing day, Mary vowed to carry the lessons of Yom Kippur in her heart, to heed the words of the prophets, and to live a life that reflected God's will. She knew that the journey of faith was ongoing, and she embraced it with the profound understanding that seeking God's grace and striving to be a vessel of love and goodness was a lifelong endeavor.

Broken Promises

On a warm summer afternoon, the three young friends, Mary, Rachael, and Hannah, embarked on an adventure to the wooded area outside of Nazareth. The scorching sun beat down on them as they walked, but the excitement of exploring the forest and seeking some relief from the heat kept their spirits high.

As they strolled along the dusty path, they couldn't help but delve into a conversation about the promises God made to various prophets and how humanity often struggled to uphold their end of the divine covenants.

"Remember what we learned in Hebrew school about the Abrahamic Covenant?" Mary asked her friends, brushing a lock of hair from her forehead.

"Yeah, God promised to bless Abraham and make him the father of a great nation," Rachael chimed in. "And through his descendants, all the nations of the earth would be blessed."

Hannah nodded in agreement, adding, "Then there's the Mosaic Covenant with the Ten Commandments and the comprehensive law code. God gave the Israelites guidance on how to live righteously and in harmony with one another."

As they continued their walk, they shared their knowledge of the other covenants they had learned in Hebrew school.

"The Davidic Covenant is fascinating," Mary said. "God promised King David that his dynasty would endure forever, and the Messiah would come from his line. That's like a promise of hope and redemption!"

"And let's not forget the New Covenant," Rachael added. "Jeremiah and Ezekiel spoke of forgiveness of sins and the indwelling of the Spirit. It shows how God's love and grace extend to everyone."

The girls found a shaded spot beneath a large oak tree in the forest and settled down. The coolness of the woods provided much-needed relief from the heat. They leaned against the tree trunk, feeling connected to nature and to the lessons they had learned about God's covenants.

"But you know," Mary said thoughtfully, "it seems like throughout history, people have struggled to keep their end of the deal with God. They often forget the promises made and turn away from living righteously. This is why every year we celebrate Yom Kippur, to atone for sins. That was only last month, remember?". The other girls giggled and said, "Of course we remember Mary!"

But Hannah nodded in agreement with Mary's comment. "It's true. Time and again, we see examples of how we fall short. Even with all these incredible promises from God, we still find ourselves making mistakes and straying from the path."

Right then, a Eurasian collared dove flew into the forest and swooped right past the girls to a nest just above them on the tree that sat near. They knew this type of dove because it was very common in Nazareth and it had a distinctive black "collar" marking on the back of its neck. The girls always would call them dirty necked doves. The swiftness of the bird flying right toward them made them wonder of God was trying to tell them something about their behavior at hope or school. But then they saw the bird feeding it's babies in the nest and knew that was why he was flying so fast.

Rachael added, "Sometimes it feels like we're repeating the same patterns as the Israelites in the wilderness. They witnessed God's miracles, yet they still grumbled and disobeyed."

The girls sat in silence for a moment, contemplating the weight of their words.

"But you know," Mary said, breaking the silence, "the covenants aren't just about what God expects from us. They also show His unending love, mercy, and faithfulness. Despite our imperfections, God continues to uphold His promises."

Hannah smiled. "That's true. The Noahic Covenant is a perfect example. God promised never to destroy the earth again with a flood, and the rainbow is a reminder of that covenant."

Rachel said "It would be nice to have a passing shower of rain right now to cool things off and so we could see a rainbow. What do you think God? If I do my chores that I did too quickly this morning and do them the right way, will you give us a rainbow?". The three girls laughed, but Mary said that we shouldn't mock our relationship with God like that.

"Yes, I know that, Mary. I am sorry God! Let's see, what other covenants did we learn about? Oh yeah, the Covenant with Phinehas," Rachael added, "God honored Phinehas and his descendants with an everlasting priesthood because of Phinehas's zealousness for God's honor. It shows that God rewards those who are devoted to Him."

Mary nodded. "Exactly. The covenants are a reflection of God's unchanging character and His desire for a loving relationship with us."

As the sun began to lower in the western sky, the girls felt a sense of peace and wonder envelop them. The forest seemed to whisper stories of ancient times and divine promises. The importance of living in accordance with God's laws and cherishing the covenant relationship with Him became even more evident.

Hand in hand, the friends began their journey back to their homes, their hearts filled with newfound understanding and gratitude. The promises God made to the prophets were not just tales of the past; they were living truths that resonated in their lives and the world around them.

As they walked, they knew that they would continue to seek God's guidance and strive to uphold the covenant relationship with Him.

They were determined to live with righteousness, compassion, and humility, knowing that even amidst human frailty, God's love and providence would forever endure.

Mary came to the split in the road, where she lived one way and Hannah and Rachel lived the others so they said goodbye and hugged each other. It is so good to have such good friends. Mary made her way back home from her afternoon in the forest. The laughter and chatter of her friends still echoed in her mind, but amidst the joy, a nagging question lingered: How could one truly know if their repentance and atonement for grave sins were enough?

Arriving home, Mary was welcomed with open arms by her parents, Anne and Joachim. They sat together at the dinner table, breaking bread and sharing stories of their day. Mary felt a sense of comfort in their presence, yet she couldn't shake the weight of her thoughts about sin and forgiveness.

After the meal, as the evening prayers began, Mary's mind wandered back to the stories she had learned in Hebrew school, stories of repentance that had resonated with her.

"Mom, Dad," Mary finally mustered the courage to speak, "Please do not grow weary with all my questions about these things. I still don't quite understand how one can be sure that their repentance and sacrifices are enough for really serious sins against God's covenants."

Anne and Joachim exchanged a knowing glance, recognizing the depth of their daughter's question. "Mary," Anne began gently, "repentance is not merely about following a set formula or offering sacrifices. It's about a genuine change of heart and turning away from sin."

Joachim added, "In the stories of the people of Nineveh, David, and the Israelites in the wilderness, we see that true repentance involves recognizing one's wrongdoing, feeling genuine remorse, and seeking God's forgiveness with a humble heart."

Mary nodded, absorbing their words, but still, a hint of uncertainty lingered. "But what if the sins are so great? Like the wickedness of King Manasseh or the idolatrous practices of King Ahab? Can God's mercy truly extend to such depths of darkness?"

Anne smiled, her eyes reflecting wisdom and compassion. "My dear, the scriptures show us that God's mercy knows no bounds. King Manasseh's repentance, despite his grave sins, moved God to show him mercy. And King Ahab, even after his evil deeds, was granted forgiveness when he humbled himself before God."

Joachim chimed in, "In the story of King Josiah, we see how an entire nation repented upon rediscovering the Book of the Law. They removed idols and reformed their worship, and God accepted their heartfelt repentance."

"And after the Babylonian exile," Anne added, "the returned exiles, led by Ezra and Nehemiah, repented of their intermarriage with foreign nations and their sins. They sought God's forgiveness, and He restored them."

Listening to her parents' explanations and the examples from the scriptures, Mary felt a profound sense of relief. She began to understand that true repentance was not about earning forgiveness through acts of atonement but about opening one's heart to God's love and mercy.

As the evening prayers came to a close, Mary felt a newfound clarity and peace within her. She knew that the path of righteousness and forgiveness lay in acknowledging one's sins, feeling genuine remorse, and seeking God's mercy with a sincere heart.

In the days that followed, Mary continued to study the stories of repentance in the scriptures, finding solace in the knowledge that God's love was boundless and His forgiveness eternal. She understood that no matter how grave the sin, genuine repentance and turning to God would always lead to His merciful embrace.

With each passing day, Mary grew in her understanding of the sacred covenants between God and His people. She learned that God's promises of forgiveness and redemption were interwoven with the call to live in righteousness and love.

In her heart, Mary held a profound appreciation for the stories of repentance that had shaped her faith. She knew that the journey of seeking God's grace was one of continuous growth and learning, a path that called for humility, compassion, and a resolute commitment to living in alignment with God's will.

As she looked out the window at the starlit night, Mary felt a deep sense of gratitude for the guidance and wisdom her parents had shared. With faith as her guiding light, she knew that no matter how challenging the road ahead might be, God's love and mercy would always be there, lighting her way home.

Rachel is Very Sick

As the sun began to rise a few days later, casting a warm glow over the village of Nazareth, Mary and Hannah hurriedly made their way to Rachel's home. The news of their friend's illness had reached them late the day earlier, and they couldn't bear to see Rachel suffering but knew that they had to do something to help. Her stomach ailment had left her weak and unable to keep any food down.

Arriving at Rachel's doorstep, they were greeted by Isaac, Rachel's older brother, who had returned home from his studies in Jerusalem. He had dreams of becoming a rabbi, the first in their family to achieve such an honor. His eyes were filled with concern as he welcomed Mary and Hannah inside.

The small room was dimly lit, and Rachel lay on her bed, her face pale and pained. Isaac had been trying to ease her fever by placing a cloth soaked in cold water on her forehead. Every few minutes, she would fall into a fitful slumber, only to wake up moments later, the pain still evident in her eyes.

Seeing their friend in such distress, both Mary and Hannah couldn't help but feel an overwhelming sense of worry and helplessness. As they sat beside Rachel, their minds filled with questions about God's promises and warnings.

"Isaac," Mary began hesitantly, "we've been thinking a lot about the promises God made to our ancestors, like Abraham and the others. How can we be sure that those promises still hold true for us today? Especially with Rachel so sick right now. I have never seen her this sick."

Isaac smiled warmly, understanding the weight of their question. "You see, God's promises are timeless and eternal. When God promised Abraham that his descendants would be as numerous as the stars and that all nations would be blessed through his offspring, He meant it for all generations. It is through faith that we become the spiritual descendants of Abraham and partake in those promises."

Hannah nodded, absorbing his words. "And the promise of the land of Canaan to Abraham, Isaac, and Jacob, does that still apply to us too?"

"Absolutely," Isaac replied. "God's covenant with our ancestors included the promise of the land of Canaan as their inheritance. And though we are not physically in Canaan, the significance of that promise remains. Our spiritual inheritance is the hope of the Messianic kingdom and the everlasting kingdom of God."

As Rachel's fever persisted, Mary's voice trembled, "But what about the promise of the Messiah? When will He come, and how will we know?"

Isaac's eyes lit up with conviction. "The promise of the Messiah is at the core of our faith. Throughout the Hebrew Scriptures, there are numerous prophecies foretelling the coming of the Anointed One, the Savior who will bring salvation and establish God's everlasting kingdom. We believe that He will fulfill these prophecies and that we must remain vigilant and faithful in our waiting." He continued, "With all the evil we see today, it will be interesting to see how the Messiah will come and make himself known."

Hannah looked thoughtful. "And what about the new covenant God promised to make? The one where He would write His law on our hearts and forgive our sins?"

"That covenant was prophesied by Jeremiah," Isaac explained, "Many of us at the Temple in Jerusalem have been thinking that The Messiah will be a tall, muscular man who alone can fight off an entire army of Roman soldiers." "But we haven't figured out how He would just appear and yet be recognized as a descendant of David with a proven lineage."

The room fell silent for a moment, the weight of their questions and the promise of God's faithfulness hanging in the air.

Isaac then began to share stories from their history, reminding Mary and Hannah of the warnings God had given His people throughout the ages.

"He warned the Israelites against worshiping other gods and making idols," Isaac said. "Their disobedience led to God's judgment and discipline."

"And He warned them that if they strayed from His commandments, they would face various curses and punishments," Hannah added.

"Exactly," Isaac nodded. "But it's essential to remember that God also sent prophets to warn His people and call them to repentance. Just as He warned the people of Nineveh through Jonah, He continues to warn us when we go astray."

As the day wore on, Rachel's fever showed no signs of abating. The girls could see the exhaustion in Isaac's eyes as he left to fetch a fresh bucket of cold well water to soothe Rachel's forehead. Feeling the weight of their friend's suffering, Mary and Hannah decided to do what they had been taught from an early age: to pray fervently for healing.

Taking a deep breath, each girl held one of Rachel's hands, and they began to pray with all their hearts. They prayed for God's mercy, for His healing touch, and for Rachel's strength to return.

In that moment, as their prayers filled the room, something miraculous happened. Rachel's fever began to break, and she slowly sat up, a faint smile appearing on her face. "I'm hungry," she whispered, her voice weak but filled with hope. Isaac had just returned from the well as his sister sat up in bed.

Isaac's eyes filled with tears of gratitude as he brought some food for Rachel to eat. Mary and Hannah could hardly believe what they had witnessed, a tangible manifestation of God's love and mercy in response to their prayers.

In that sacred moment, the three friends knew that God's promises were not just words of the past, but living truths that carried immense power. His warnings were not meant to bring fear but to steer them back onto the path of righteousness.

As they shared a meal together, Mary, Hannah, Rachel and Isaac held a newfound appreciation for the depth and meaning of God's promises. The journey of faith and understanding was far from over, but they knew that their hearts would forever be anchored in the hope of God's love, mercy, and redemption. And they would face the future, knowing that in God's promises, there was an unwavering source of strength and assurance.

Maturing in so many ways

As the months turned into more than a year that followed since Rachel's sickness, Mary, Hannah, and Rachel experienced a profound transformation in their lives. Their friendship deepened, and their shared quest for spiritual growth became a driving force in their daily interactions. As they challenged each other's understanding of the Torah as well as exploring practical ways of applying its teachings, they found themselves becoming not only better friends but also stronger individuals within the community.

The trio spent countless hours together, poring over the sacred scriptures, discussing the stories of their ancestors, and pondering the lessons embedded in each narrative. They delved into the words of the prophets, seeking to discern God's messages of love, justice, and mercy.

As they studied, they began to grasp the interconnectedness of God's promises and warnings throughout history. They saw how the ancient prophecies foreshadowed the ultimate fulfillment in the coming of the Messiah. The more they learned, the more they marveled at the intricate tapestry of God's plan for His people.

In their pursuit of wisdom and righteousness, Mary, Hannah, and Rachel sought guidance from the elders and scholars of their community. They engaged in respectful debates and sometimes long discussions, challenging one another's perspectives and growing in their ability to articulate their beliefs with clarity and humility.

Their newfound knowledge was not merely intellectual; it found practical expression in their daily lives. Inspired by the teachings on social responsibility and compassion, they volunteered to help the poor and the vulnerable in their community. They visited the sick and provided comfort to those in need, embodying the principles of love and kindness.

Through their studies, they came to appreciate the significance of God's covenant with His people. The Abrahamic Covenant, the Mosaic Covenant, the Davidic Covenant – these were not just historical accounts but living promises that touched their lives. They learned that they, too, were recipients of those promises and heirs to God's blessings.

One summer day, as they sat by the clear waters of a nearby stream, the girls reflected on their journey of growth and maturation. The sun cast a golden glow on their faces, and the laughter of children playing in the distance mingled with the rustling of the leaves.

Rachel smiled, her eyes reflecting newfound wisdom. "I used to think that God's promises were just stories for our ancestors, but now I realize they are as real and applicable to us today."

Hannah nodded in agreement. "And the warnings in the scriptures are not meant to frighten us, but to guide us toward the path of righteousness and keep us from straying."

Mary added, "The more we understand God's word, the more we see the beauty of His plan for us and the entire world. Both of you hold a strong desire to find a man, get married and have a family. All this knowledge we've gained will ensure that you will both be great teachers of your children."

Hannah giggled at the thought of she and Rachel becoming mothers, but replied back to Mary, "Rachel and I both admire your new commitment to remain a virgin, Mary. This is a great sacrifice you are making, but we know you'd be the best mother of all of us, if the Lord willed it."

Their hearts swelled with gratitude for the opportunity to learn and grow together. They were no longer mere girls but young women on a shared journey of faith and self-discovery. As they continued to explore the depths of the Torah, they found strength in their unity and the assurance that they were never alone in their pursuit of truth and righteousness.

As the seasons changed and another year passed, they knew that their spiritual journey was far from over. There was still much to learn, and they looked forward to facing the challenges and triumphs that lay ahead.

One evening, as they sat under the starlit sky, Mary, Hannah, and Rachel joined hands in a moment of silence, offering their gratitude to God for the lessons learned, the joys shared, and the growth they had experienced together.

"We are bound by something more profound than friendship," Rachel said softly. "We are bound by our shared love for God and His word."

Hannah nodded, a tear of joy glistening in her eye. "And as we continue on this journey, let us remember to be a light to others and share the wisdom we have gained."

Mary smiled, feeling the warmth of their bond. "Let's always challenge and encourage one another to be the best versions of ourselves, just as iron sharpens iron."

In that moment of unity and commitment, Mary, Hannah, and Rachel knew that their friendship was a gift from God, guiding them to live with purpose and intention. They were no longer just girls from Nazareth; they were bearers of hope, love, and understanding in a world longing for God's light.

As they gazed at the night sky, they felt a deep sense of peace and wonder. They knew that their journey had just begun and that the road ahead would be filled with trials and triumphs, but they were ready to face it all together, strengthened by their love for one another and their shared devotion to the teachings of the Torah.

And so, as the stars twinkled above them, Mary, Hannah, and Rachel embraced the future with open hearts and a steadfast commitment to living lives that honored God and brought light to the world around them. Their journey of growth and maturation would continue, guided by God's promises and illuminated by the enduring flame of their friendship.

They navigated the challenges of adolescence and the uncertainties of life with unwavering support for one another. Each step they took in their individual journeys was intertwined with the shared understanding of God's promises and warnings.

Their studies and discussions of the Torah became a foundation for their decisions, actions, and relationships. As they matured emotionally, spiritually, and physically, they found solace and guidance in the sacred texts. The wisdom they gained from the scriptures fueled their compassion for others and deepened their commitment to living according to God's commandments.

The young women's faith not only influenced their own lives but also radiated to those around them. People in the community noticed the positive impact of their friendship and their dedication to helping those in need. As they offered a listening ear to the troubled, comfort to the grieving, and kindness to the marginalized, Mary, Hannah, and Rachel became beacons of light in the midst of life's challenges.

One particular summer day, as the sun bathed the fields of Nazareth in warmth, the three friends decided to embark on a special project together. They had learned about the plight of widows and orphans in their community, and their hearts were moved to make a difference.

Pooling their resources and talents, they started a small support group for widows, offering practical help, companionship, and encouragement. They also reached out to the children who had lost their parents, organizing gatherings to provide a sense of belonging and support during difficult times.

As they worked tirelessly on this endeavor, their actions mirrored the covenant principles they had learned from the Torah. They were fulfilling the call to protect the vulnerable and care for those in need, becoming living examples of God's love in action.

Their dedication to social responsibility and community service brought them into contact with people from different walks of life. They met individuals who were struggling and others who had lost hope. Their hearts were burdened, and they sought ways to bring comfort and hope to those around them.

As Mary, Hannah, and Rachel continued to serve others, they discovered that their lives were richly blessed by the relationships they forged. Each encounter became an opportunity to learn and grow, deepening their understanding of God's grace and the power of repentance.

Isaac Returns to Nazareth

In the warm glow of a Nazareth evening, the small community gathered eagerly in the courtyard of the local synagogue. Excitement filled the air as they awaited the return of Isaac, Rachel's older brother, who had been away in Jerusalem for years, studying to become a rabbi. The news of his imminent arrival had spread like wildfire, and people from neighboring villages had also come to witness this momentous occasion.

Among the crowd were Mary and Rachel, their eyes shining with anticipation. Both girls had grown into young women, and they shared a special bond with Isaac, who had always been like an older brother to Mary and Hannah as much as he was a real brother to Rachel. They had studied together as children, and Isaac's wisdom and knowledge had been a source of inspiration for both Mary and Rachel.

As the sun dipped below the horizon, a murmur of excitement spread through the crowd as Isaac appeared at the entrance of the synagogue. He was now a grown man, with a beard adorning his face, a symbol of his scholarly pursuits. The people welcomed him with warm smiles and heartfelt greetings, and he humbly acknowledged their affection.

With a gentle smile, Isaac addressed the crowd, "My friends, it warms my heart to see all of you gathered here today. I have returned from Jerusalem with a deep sense of purpose and a burning desire to share the knowledge I have acquired during my studies."

I want to start by sharing with you the words from the prophet Isaiah in a manner different than how you've heard his words interpreted before. We have longed for our Messiah since Father Abraham. But many of the words of Isaiah have been glossed over by many teachers of Scriptures. I have my sister Rachel and her best friends Mary and Hannah to thank for encouraging me to dig deeply into the words of Isaiah to understand the true meaning, and I have confirmed with my own teachers and other scripture scholars that what I am about to say is true.

The people listened intently as Isaac began to read from the scriptures. He started with Isaiah's prophesy to King Ahaz, "Therefore the Lord himself will give you a sign: The virgin will conceive and give birth to a son, and will call him Immanuel. He will be eating curds and honey when he knows enough to reject the wrong and choose the right, for before the boy knows enough to reject the wrong and choose the right, the land of the two kings you dread will be laid waste."

As he continued, he read from more from the Prophet Isaiah, "For to us, a child is born, to us, a son is given, and the government will be on his shoulders. And he will be called Wonderful Counselor, Mighty God, Everlasting Father, Prince of Peace. Of the greatness of his government and peace, there will be no end." Isaac raised his finger into the air, saying "He will reign on David's throne and over his kingdom,

establishing and upholding it with justice and righteousness from that time on and forever."

Isaac paused for it to start to sink in, then said, "Isaiah told us clearly that there will be a great sign – that the sign will be a son of the house of David; would be born to a virgin; and that son will be God Himself!"

The words of the prophet Isaiah filled the air, resonating deeply within the hearts of the listeners. But then, Isaac turned to further into the words of Isaiah to a passage that spoke of a suffering servant, and a hush fell over the crowd as they listened intently.

He was despised and rejected by mankind, a man of suffering, and
familiar with pain.

Like one from whom people hide their faces he was despised, and we held him in low esteem.
Surely, he took up our pain and bore our suffering, yet we considered him punished by God,
stricken by him, and afflicted. But he was pierced for our transgressions, he was crushed for our iniquities; the punishment that brought us peace was on him,
and by his wounds we are healed. We all, like sheep, have gone astray, each of us has turned to our own way; and the Lord has laid on him the iniquity of us all.
He was oppressed and afflicted, yet he did not open his mouth; he was led like a lamb to the slaughter,
and as a sheep before its shearers is silent, so he did not open his mouth.
By oppression and judgment he was taken away. Yet who of his generation protested?
For he was cut off from the land of the living; for the transgression of my people he was punished.
He was assigned a grave with the wicked, and with the rich in his death, though he had done no violence, nor was any deceit in his mouth.
Yet it was the Lord's will to crush him and cause him to suffer, and though the Lord makes his life an offering for sin, he will see his offspring and prolong his days, and the will of the Lord will prosper in his hand.
After he has suffered, he will see the light of life and be satisfied; by his knowledge
my righteous servant will justify many, and he will bear their iniquities.
Therefore I will give him a portion among the great, and he will divide the spoils with the strong,
because he poured out his life unto death, and was numbered with the transgressors.
For he bore the sin of many, and made intercession for the transgressors.

Isaac paused and looked at the faces before him, his eyes meeting those of Mary and Rachel. "My dear friends," he said, his voice filled with compassion, "these scriptures hold a profound truth that speaks of a Messiah who will suffer for the sake of others. The Messiah will bear the burden of our sins and bring us peace through his sacrifice."

The crowd listened in rapt attention, captivated by Isaac's words and the depth of his understanding. He went on to explain the concept of the suffering servant, the significance of atonement, and the role of the Messiah as a source of hope and redemption.

As the evening wore on, Isaac continued to teach and share his insights from the scriptures. His words touched the hearts of the people, and many were moved to tears by the profound truths he revealed. Some of them were struggling to understand how someone who would be their savior could be subject to such pain and suffering.

Mary and Rachel listened with awe and admiration for Isaac. They knew that his return to Nazareth marked the beginning of a new chapter in his life, one where he would be recognized as a rabbi and a leader in the community.

As the night sky sparkled with stars, the gathering slowly dispersed, each person carrying the wisdom and teachings of Isaac in their hearts. Mary and Rachel walked back home together, their minds buzzing with the revelations they had just experienced.

"We are witnessing something truly special," Mary said, her eyes shining with reverence. "Isaac's knowledge and understanding of the scriptures are awe-inspiring."

Rachel nodded; her heart filled with pride for her brother. "Indeed, his words have opened my eyes to the deeper meaning of the scriptures. The Messiah's suffering holds such profound significance."

"We must continue to learn from him," Mary replied. "And we must share this knowledge with others, just as he has shared it with us."

Isaac's Friend

In the bustling town of Nazareth, the warm sun bathed the cobblestone streets as Isaac settled into the house of his childhood friend, Joseph. Both in their early twenties, they had reunited after years of being apart, and their friendship quickly rekindled. Joseph, a skilled carpenter and stone mason, proudly showed Isaac the craftsmanship of his work, and Isaac, in turn, shared his knowledge of scriptures and the prophecies he had studied in Jerusalem.

As the days passed, Isaac invited Joseph to join him at the synagogue to hear him speak about the profound prophecies found in the Hebrew scriptures. Together, they sat among the congregation of Nazareth, and Isaac passionately expounded on the words of the prophet Hosea.

"Hear me, my dear friends," Isaac began, his voice clear and resonant. "In the words of Hosea, we find a powerful testament of God's love for Israel, even in times of unfaithfulness. Despite our failings, God yearns for our return, and He foretells a future of restoration and reconciliation."

The people listened attentively as Isaac quoted Hosea's words, conveying the depth of God's love and His longing for the repentance of His people. His insights illuminated the meaning behind the ancient text, inspiring hope and stirring hearts.

As the days passed, Isaac continued to share his knowledge of other prophecies with Joseph as well as Joseph's younger brother Cleopas. Together, they explored the words of the prophet Micah, who foretold that the Messiah would be born in Bethlehem and would come to shepherd His people with love and compassion. When Isaac mentioned Bethlehem to Joseph and Cleopas, their ears perked up. They said that Bethlehem was the town of their ancestral home, closely associated with King David. Isaac was surprised that the name Bethlehem meant "House of Bread". They all marveled at the intricacies of God's plan, woven through the fabric of time and prophecy.

That night as they arrived at the synagogue courtyard, Isaac introduced Cleopas and Joseph to Rachel, Mary and Hannah before they took these places inside. Isaac shared the same prophecies of Micah which he told Joseph and Cleopas about and even got into the stories of Zechariah, with its themes of restoration and salvation. Isaac explained how these prophecies pointed to the coming of the Messiah, who would bring healing and hope to a broken world. He even pointed out to the crowd that Joseph and Cleopas' ancestral home of Bethlehem meant "House of Bread". Mary, Rachel and Hannah were happy that Isaac's talk tonight was filled with so much more hope about the Messiah than the preaching from the night before.

As they walked into the courtyard after their evening of study, Joseph shyly walked up to Mary and asked her if she would like to sit and talk. Mary accepted his invitation. Joseph talked about how much he enjoyed Isaac's talk tonight, but more importantly, he was happy to meet her. Mary began to blush and said that she noticed him looking at her throughout the evening talk. Joseph said, "Now Mary, how could you have noticed how much I was looking at you, if you were not looking over at me?"

Mary replied, "Joseph, you tricked me, but yes, I was looking at you. You are a strong man; you have great skills working with your hands to create homes for people. Any single woman would dream of a man like you. Because you are such good friends with Rachel's brother Isaac, speaks volumes about your character."

Joseph quickly responded "I would like to meet you father and your mother and asked them permission to court you. Is that alright with you?"

Mary responded, "I know that they would love to meet you, but Joseph, I must tell you something. You might not want to talk to me after I tell you. הקדשתי את עצמי לאלוהים במהלך חיי בתולים *(which means "I have consecrated myself to God thru a lifetime of virginity")."*

Joseph coughed and paused for a minute. His elbows on his knees and hands folded in prayer up to his forehead, he then said "If your parents accept me, then I, too will consecrate myself to God thru my own virginity". Mary closed her eyes as if in deep thanksgiving, then twisted around and hugged Joseph.

Mary said, "come to my home for dinner tomorrow. You will meet my parents and they will love you!"

The next day, Joseph felt a mix of excitement and nervousness as he prepared to meet Mary's parents. He dressed in his best attire, wanting to make a good impression. As he approached their home, he couldn't help but wonder what kind of reception he would receive. He took a deep breath, reminding himself of his commitment to God and the love he felt for Mary, which gave him strength and courage.

When Joseph arrived at Mary's house, he was warmly welcomed by her parents, who greeted him with smiles and open arms. They were a kind and loving couple, and Joseph immediately felt at ease in their presence. They sat down for dinner, and Mary's mother served a delicious meal that she had prepared with love.

Throughout the dinner, Joseph and Mary's parents engaged in heartfelt conversations. Joseph shared stories of his faith journey and his desire to lead a life dedicated to God. He spoke about his upbringing, the values instilled in him by his parents, and his dreams for the future. Mary's parents were impressed by Joseph's sincerity and the depth of his devotion.

When the time felt right, Joseph mustered up the courage to express his intentions. He turned to Mary's father and said, "Sir, I would be honored if you would allow me to court your daughter Mary. I promise to cherish and respect her, and to always prioritize her happiness and well-being."

Mary's father exchanged a glance with his wife, and then he smiled warmly at Joseph. "You seem like a fine young man, and it's evident that you genuinely care for our Mary," he said. "We trust our daughter's judgment, and if she has chosen you, then we give our blessing to your courtship."

Mary's mother nodded in agreement, adding, "We can see that your faith is important to you, and we appreciate the respect you have shown by sharing your intentions with us. May God guide your path together."

Joseph felt a wave of relief and gratitude wash over him. He thanked Mary's parents for their trust and acceptance, knowing that this was the beginning of a significant chapter in his life. He glanced at Mary, who had tears of joy in her eyes, and he couldn't help but smile back at her.

Over the following weeks and months, Joseph and Mary's courtship flourished, deepening their bond and love for one another. They shared their dreams, their fears, and their unwavering faith. Together, they grew stronger in their commitment to God and to each other.

As they navigated the challenges and joys of their courtship, they always carried with them the mutual understanding of their shared commitment to living a life of consecration to God through their virginity. It became a beautiful and profound aspect of their relationship, fostering an unbreakable connection built on faith, trust, and selflessness.

Their love story inspired those around them, and their devotion to God and each other became a beacon of hope and love in their community. Joseph and Mary's courtship marked the beginning of a lifelong journey together, filled with blessings, challenges, and the unwavering knowledge that their love was rooted in a sacred bond with God.

One evening, as the setting sun painted the sky with hues of orange and pink, Rachel, Hannah, Isaac, Joseph, and Mary sat under the shade of a fig tree in Joseph's garden. The air was filled with the sweet aroma of blossoms, and the sound of birds singing in the distance created a serene atmosphere.

Isaac spoke about the prophecies of Isaiah, describing the Messiah's role as a light to the nations and the fulfillment of God's promise to His people. As he spoke, Joseph couldn't help but glance at Mary, her eyes fixed intently on Isaac, absorbing every word he said.

A soft smile played on Mary's lips as she noticed Joseph's gaze, and in that moment, they both felt a deep connection, grounded in their shared faith and spiritual journey. Mary admired Joseph's reverence for God's word and his unwavering commitment to his craft, and Joseph was drawn to Mary's gentle spirit and the way she radiated grace and kindness.

As the evening wore on, the group continued to explore the prophecies, and Mary and Joseph found themselves drawn to each other, their hearts entwined by a shared love for God and His promises.

In the weeks that followed, Mary and Joseph spent more time together, attending synagogue gatherings and joining Isaac in his discussions about the scriptures. They supported each other in their spiritual quests and found solace in their shared beliefs.

Through their shared journey of faith and understanding, Mary and Joseph's affection for each other grew stronger. Yet, in their commitment to living virtuously, they knew that their love would need to be expressed in other ways that give glory and honor to God, bringing their friends and the community closer to God in anticipation of the coming of the Messiah.

And so, in the quaint town of Nazareth, a profound love story unfolded—not only between Mary and Joseph but also between friends bound by their shared journey of discovering God's truth and His unwavering promises. It was a love that would shape their destinies and play a pivotal role in the unfolding of God's grand plan for all of humanity.

The Invitation

The morning sun cast a golden glow over the hills of Nazareth as it peeked through Mary's window. She woke up with a smile, feeling slightly older and more responsible, even at the tender age of 14. She stretched and yawned, appreciating the cool morning breeze that filled her room. As she closed the window, she could hear the cheerful chirping of birds and the familiar sound of sheep bleating in the distance.

The inviting scent of freshly baked bread wafted from the kitchen, and Mary hurried downstairs to find her mother, Anne, preparing breakfast. The warm smile on her mother's face welcomed her, and Mary gladly accepted the bowl of steaming porridge topped with honey and nuts. She savored each spoonful, the sweetness bringing comfort to her hunger.

After breakfast, Mary and her mother recited the Birkat Ha-Mazon together, expressing their gratitude to God for the blessings in their lives. With a sense of fulfillment, Mary helped her mother with the daily household tasks, taking pride in contributing to their home. As they worked side by side, they shared laughter and stories, strengthening the bond between mother and daughter.

Excited to start the day with her friends, Mary rushed outside to meet Rachel and Hannah. Their friendship had blossomed over the years, and they were inseparable. Together, they engaged in games that Jewish girls of their age enjoyed, such as playing with tops, singing traditional songs, and discussing passages from the Torah. They also practiced embroidery and shared stories about the great women of their heritage.

In the midst of their play, Mary couldn't help but share her excitement about Joseph courting her. She told Rachel and Hannah about the dinner they had with her parents and how Joseph had expressed his dedication to God through a lifetime of virginity, just as Mary had consecrated herself. Rachel and Hannah listened attentively, offering their support and encouragement.

Meanwhile, not far away, Mary's father, Joachim, observed the girls with a smile. He appreciated the bond that had formed among them and admired Mary's strong character and faith. He knew that Joseph was a fine young man, and he trusted his daughter's judgment.

As the girls played and chatted, they talked about their dreams and aspirations, imagining the possibilities that lay ahead. They supported and encouraged each other, knowing that they could rely on one another through thick and thin. In their little world of friendship and dreams, the future seemed bright and full of promise.

As the day continued, Mary suggested that they walk over to where Joseph was building a house for a young couple with a child with a deformity of the legs. The father of the boy, Levi was busy helping Joseph while Esther cared for the needs of little Yaakov in the tent nearby, their temporary home. They were excited to see Joseph, although Mary told them not to let on that she and Joseph were courting each other. Joseph looked at Mary and he knew that she had told them their secret.

Mary suggested that she, Rachel and Hannah could gather the scraps of wood from the windows and the door and gather them for the camp fire in front of the tent. The nights were starting to get cool and Yaakov shouldn't get chilled by the night air. They told Levi that they knew where there were a couple of fallen trees in the forest where they could break off some of the branches from the next day to bring to them for the fire. Hannah and Rachel said that they would go get some right then, but Mary had promised her mother that she would be home early to help prepare supper.

Her mother, Anne, had prepared for Mary a sack of fresh figs and grapes, which she gave to Levi and Esther, except for a handful she shared with Joseph. Mary said goodbye to Joseph and Levi and started walking along the path to go home.

After she returned home, Mary realized her mother must have gone to buy some of the ingredients for supper. Mary went into the small prayer room, where she began to recite the mid-day prayer, thanking God for his love and guidance. Mary felt a sense of calm wash over her as she spoke the familiar words, feeling the weight of the day's worries lift from her shoulders.

The wind picked up, lifting some dry dust from outside the window in the swirling wind around her. She shielded her eyes and mouth as best as she could with her hands. Just as quickly as the wind stirred, it stopped. As Mary lowered her hands from her face, she was stunned to see a bright light shining around her. She was filled with fear and confusion, not knowing what was happening. She could make out the profile of someone in the bright light walking toward her. And then, he spoke to her, his name was Gabriel. His face shining with a divine light, his words filled her with shock and awe.

"Mary, do not be afraid, for you have found favor with God," the he said. He told Mary that she was full of grace. She didn't understand what Gabriel was saying to her. He said that God knew that she was promised in marriage to Joseph, but God had sent him to ask her a very important question. The angel told Mary that she would have a son, whom she was to name Jesus. The angel said, "He will be great and will be called the Son of the Most High God."

Mary said "how this could be as I am a consecrated virgin". The angel answered, "The Holy Spirit will come on you, and God's power will rest on you". She couldn't believe what she was hearing. She thought to herself "Why had God chosen me, a simple girl from

Nazareth, to be the mother of his Son?" She felt overwhelmed by the weight of this responsibility, and she didn't know if she was ready for it.

Gabriel's response came with a reassurance that transcended human understanding. "The Holy Spirit will come upon you, and the power of the Most High will overshadow you. The child to be born will be holy; he will be called the Son of God."

As the angel's words sank in, Mary's mind raced. She knew the prophecies and had studied the sacred scriptures diligently. She knew that the Messiah was destined to bring salvation to the world, but she also knew that he would suffer for humanity's sins. The weight of this realization burdened her heart.

"I understand the magnitude of this mission," Mary said, her voice trembling with emotion, "but I am only human. How can I bear witness to the suffering and sacrifice of my own son?"

Gabriel's gaze softened with compassion as he replied, "Fear not, Mary, for the grace of God will be with you. Though your journey may be filled with trials, the Lord will strengthen you and guide you through every moment. Your love and faith will be your pillars of strength and an example to all who suffer."

He also told Mary that her much older cousin Elizabeth was six months pregnant, for there is nothing that God cannot do. With a gentle and reassuring voice, he told her that she had been chosen because of her faith and devotion to God, and that he would be with her every step of the way. Mary replied, "I am the Lord's servant, let it be done according to His Will".

Mary felt a sense of peace wash over her. She knew that she could trust in God's plan, and that he would give her the strength and courage to fulfill the incredible task that he had given her. In that divine encounter, Mary found solace in the presence of the angel and the knowledge that God had chosen her because of her steadfast faith and purity of heart. With newfound courage, she surrendered to the will of the Almighty, embracing her divine mission with grace and humility.

And so, She said yes to God's plan, and from that moment on, her life was forever changed. Mary knew that she would face challenges and difficulties, but she also knew that God was with her, guiding her every step of the way.

From that day forward, Mary embarked on a profound journey, nurturing the unborn Christ within her womb with love and devotion. Throughout her son's life, she knew she would witness his miraculous deeds and teachings and would treasure every moment which would somehow offset the troubling times she knew they would have to endure.

As for her, she will always cherish the moment when the archangel Gabriel appeared to her in Nazareth, and told her that she had found favor with God. It was a moment of divine revelation, one that filled her with both fear and awe.

Sleepless nights

In the tranquil courtyard of the synagogue, the sun dipped below the horizon, casting a warm, golden glow over the gathered worshippers. Mary stood at the edge of the courtyard, her heart both hopeful and apprehensive. She had agreed to meet Joseph there before evening services to share a moment of private conversation that wouldn't raise eyebrows or spark scandal among their community.

As Joseph approached, Mary's heart quickened. She admired his quiet strength and kindness, traits that had drawn her closer to him over time. They exchanged polite greetings, and then Mary gathered her courage to share her extraordinary encounter with Joseph.

"Joseph," she began, her voice trembling slightly, "I must tell you something that I believe will change both of our lives forever. Earlier today, I was visited by an angel named Gabriel, a messenger from God."

Joseph looked taken aback, his eyes widening in surprise. "An angel?" he questioned, trying to wrap his mind around the revelation.

"Yes," Mary affirmed, taking a deep breath. "The angel told me that my much older cousin, Elizabeth, who lives in Ein Karim with her husband, Zachariah, is six months pregnant and will need help with chores and the baby's delivery. I have decided to leave for her home tomorrow to assist her."

She paused for a moment, gathering her thoughts before continuing, "But that's not all. The angel also told me that I have found favor with God and that He wants me to be the mother of the Savior."

Joseph's eyebrows furrowed, and he looked perplexed. "The mother of the Savior?" he echoed, his mind grappling with the enormity of what Mary was telling him.

"Yes," Mary affirmed gently, her eyes filled with faith. "I know this is a lot to take in, but I believe the angel was sent by God, and I trust His plan for my life. I understand if this is overwhelming for you. Please, take your time to pray about it and seek guidance from the Almighty."

Joseph nodded, his mind swirling with a mix of emotions. He appreciated Mary's honesty and sincerity, but the weight of this revelation was immense. He promised her that he would indeed pray about it, seeking clarity and understanding in the stillness of the night.

That night, Joseph retreated to a quiet place to pray fervently about the situation. He poured out his heart to God, seeking wisdom and direction. Half the night passed, and his heart remained heavy with the enormity of the decision he had to make.

As weariness finally overcame him, Joseph drifted into a restless sleep. In his dreams, he saw an angel bathed in a heavenly light, standing before him. The angel spoke with a gentle authority, saying, "Joseph, son of David, do not be afraid to take Mary into your home as your wife, for the child conceived in her womb is from the Holy Spirit. He will save his people from their sins."

Awakening startled from the vision, Joseph felt a profound sense of peace and clarity. He knew in his heart that this dream was not a mere figment of his imagination but a divine message guiding him on the right path. He lit a lantern and walked in the predawn darkness to Anne and Joachim's house in hope of talking to them about his new intentions with Mary.

As the morning sun broke across the hillside of Nazareth, Joseph heard the stirrings within Mary's house. He knocked on the door and Joachim opened the door. Joachim said "Joseph, it is early, we just woke up. Is everything OK?"

Joseph said "Yes, sir, it is wonderful! I am in love with Mary! I know she will be leaving soon for Ein Karim, but I wanted to tell you that when she returns, with your permission, I would like to take her as my wife."

Joachim embraced Joseph and said, "you have my permission! Now, please come in and ask Mary and have some breakfast."

With that, the two went in. Anne saw Joachim's eyes opened wide with Joy and knew something good was about to happen. Mary walked into the room and Joseph dropped onto one knee, taking ahold of Mary's hand and said, "Mary, I love you with all my heart and want you to be my wife." Mary jumped into his arms and said "yes!". Anne and Joachim each grabbed a metal pan and a spoon and began pounding on it with joy and celebration.

Tears of joy welled up in Mary's eyes, and she embraced Joseph tightly. They knew that their journey ahead would be filled with challenges and uncertainties, but they also understood that they had been chosen for a divine purpose.

After they ate, they knew that had to get Mary to the caravan of people headed south. It would be at least a 15 hour walk each day for two days to get to Ein Karem. Joseph wanted to go with her to protect her but Mary told him she would be alright. She wanted him to finish the home he was building for Levi and Esther so he could start building a home for them!

So they said their goodbyes and Mary set off for Jaba', about half way to Ein Karim.

The Miraculous Encounter

In the small village of Ein Karim, nestled among lush hills, lived Elizabeth and her husband, Zachariah. They were a middle-aged couple, known for their devout faith and righteousness. Elizabeth had longed for a child for many years, but it seemed that her dream would remain unfulfilled.

One day about six months into her pregnancy, as Elizabeth went about her daily chores, a gentle knock on the door interrupted her thoughts. Curious, she opened the door and was met with a heartwarming sight. There, standing before her, was her young cousin, Mary, with a radiant smile on her face.

"Mary!" Elizabeth exclaimed, embracing her younger cousin warmly. "It's been too long since we last saw each other. Come, come inside."

As they sat down, Mary shared her incredible news with Elizabeth. She told her about the angel Gabriel's visit and the divine message she had received. Elizabeth listened intently, her heart filling with awe and wonder. The realization of the miracle that was unfolding before her was overwhelming.

"I, too, have received a miraculous blessing," Elizabeth revealed, her eyes shining with joy. "After all these years of barrenness, God has granted me a child. I am six months pregnant!"

Mary's face lit up with delight, and she exclaimed, "Truly, the Lord's hand is upon both of us. What a gift from God!"

At that very moment, something extraordinary happened. Elizabeth's unborn child leaped with joy within her womb, and she felt a surge of divine energy coursing through her. She placed her hands gently on her belly, marveling at the sensation.

"Did you feel that?" Elizabeth asked Mary, her heart overflowing with awe.

"Yes," Mary replied, her eyes shining with wonder. "It's as if your child knows and acknowledges the presence of the Savior within me."

Elizabeth nodded, understanding the profound significance of the moment. "Indeed," she said, "Our sons are destined for a divine purpose. Your child will be the Savior, the Son of God, and my son, John, will prepare the way for Him."

As the days passed, Mary stayed with Elizabeth and Zachariah, providing companionship and assistance. The two women spent hours in conversation, delving into the mysteries of God's plan for their children and the role they would play in bringing salvation to the world.

As the days turned into weeks, Mary and Elizabeth's bond deepened as they shared their hopes and fears about the divine calling bestowed upon them. In the quiet moments of the evening, they poured over sacred scriptures, seeking solace and guidance in God's word.

One evening, as the sun set over the horizon, casting a warm glow over the village, Mary and Elizabeth sat under the ancient olive tree in the courtyard. The air was filled with the fragrance of blossoms, and a gentle breeze rustled the leaves overhead.

"Elizabeth, I can't help but feel overwhelmed by the magnitude of what is happening," Mary confided, her eyes reflecting her vulnerability.

Elizabeth placed a reassuring hand on Mary's shoulder and said, "I understand, dear cousin. We have been chosen for a divine purpose, one that surpasses our understanding. But remember, God's hand is upon us, and He will guide us every step of the way."

"I know," Mary replied, "but I worry about the sufferings that my child will have to endure. The angel spoke of the Savior's sacrifice for the sins of humanity."

Elizabeth nodded; her gaze fixed on the distant horizon. "Yes, the scriptures speak of the Messiah's suffering. It is a weighty burden, but we must trust in God's plan. Your child, like mine, is part of a divine tapestry that will bring salvation to the world."

As Elizabeth's due date neared, the village of Ein Karim buzzed with excitement, as a woman her age certainly never produces a child! The birth of her long-awaited son was a testament to God's faithfulness and grace. Mary stayed by her side, offering comfort and encouragement during the final days of her pregnancy.

One evening, as they sat by the hearth, Elizabeth shared stories of her husband Zachariah's encounter with the angel Gabriel. "When he received the news of John's impending birth," she said, "Zachariah was struck with disbelief. He questioned how it could be possible at our age. But the angel silenced him, and Zachariah lost his ability to speak until our son was born and we name him John."

Mary listened attentively, marveling at the wonder of divine intervention. "It's truly a miraculous journey we're on," she said, "and I am grateful to share it with you, Elizabeth."

In the days that followed, Mary found strength and comfort in the peaceful presence of her older cousin. They laughed together, shared meals, and prayed fervently for the future that lay ahead.

As Elizabeth's time to give birth drew near, the atmosphere in Ein Karim was filled with anticipation. The village women gathered around to support and assist her during the momentous event. Mary stood at her side, offering words of encouragement and love.

When the day finally arrived, the village seemed to hold its breath in excitement. Elizabeth's labor was long and arduous, but she endured with unwavering faith. In the midst of pain and struggle, she found solace in the knowledge that her son's destiny was divinely ordained.

At last, the cries of a newborn baby filled the air. Elizabeth's eyes brimmed with tears of joy as she held her son for the first time. "Welcome, little John," she whispered, "a child of promise and purpose."

As the news of John's birth spread through the village, Mary and Elizabeth found themselves surrounded by friends and family, rejoicing in the miracle that had taken place. Amidst the celebration, Mary could not help but think of the future and the path that awaited her own child.

In the following days, Mary prepared to return to Nazareth. The time had come for her to continue her own journey, to join Joseph in marriage, knowing that she would soon give birth to the Son of God. The conversations she had shared with Elizabeth were etched in her heart, a wellspring of strength as she faced the uncertainties ahead.

Before her departure, Mary sat with Elizabeth once more, their hearts heavy with the knowledge of the sacrifices their sons would make. They turned to the scriptures once again, finding comfort in the words of the prophets that foretold the Messiah's sufferings.

"Our sons' destinies are intertwined," Elizabeth said, "John's mission is to prepare the way for the Savior, to announce His coming to the world. And your son, Mary, will be the One who saves humanity from sin."

Mary nodded, her gaze fixed on the horizon, her heart brimming with faith. "I will cherish every moment with my child," she said, "even in the face of pain and sacrifice, I know that God's love will sustain us."

Focus on Mary

The news of Elizabeth's miraculous birth spread like wildfire through the Judean countryside, echoing from village to village and reaching the ears of those near and far. The tale of an older, barren woman giving birth to a son filled hearts with wonder and amazement. People gathered in marketplaces and by wells, sharing in the story of divine intervention.

Joseph received word of the miraculous event while in Nazareth, and his heart swelled with a mixture of excitement and urgency. Without hesitation, he packed his belongings and set off on a journey to Ein Karim, where Elizabeth and Zachariah resided.

As Joseph's steps carried him closer to Ein Karim, his mind was filled with thoughts of Mary and the miraculous child growing within her womb. The realization of their divine connection warmed his heart, and he longed to see his beloved soon.

He arrived in after sunrise in Ein Karim, at the house of Zachariah and Elizabeth at a surprise to Mary. She, Elizabeth and the baby, John, were in the garden talking. She thought that she would have to make the 30-hour trip alone again, but Joseph said she would never be left alone again. Joseph had brought along a cart filled with straw to be not only a cushion for Mary, but also to provide food for the donkey which pulled it.

After Joseph watered the donkey and splashed some water on his face after his own walk thru the night, they said their goodbyes to Elizabeth, Zachariah and baby John and set off for Jaba' where they would spend the night before traveling on to Nazareth.

Zachariah clasped Joseph's hand firmly. "You are chosen to protect and care for Mary and the child she carries," he said. "May God guide your steps."

With their blessings and prayers, Joseph and Mary set off on their journey to Nazareth. The path before them was challenging, but their hearts were filled with faith and hope.

As Joseph and Mary traversed the rugged terrain, they cherished every moment together. At times, they held hands as they walked, their fingers interlocked with a love that knew no bounds, but when the road was made smooth, Mary sat in the cart and rested her legs

They shared stories of their childhood and the dreams they had nurtured in their hearts. They spoke of their encounters with angels and the profound sense of purpose that had enveloped them.

They sang songs of praise and offered prayers of gratitude for the miracles that had brought them together. In the quiet moments of the evening outside of Jaba', they sat by the fire and gazed at the stars, pondering the wonders of God's creation.

In the morning, Joseph made sure Mary was well-rested and nourished with all the food Elizabeth packed for them for the trip. He cared for her with tenderness and love, knowing that they were not alone on this journey. He sensed the divine presence guiding their path, and his heart was filled with awe and gratitude.

Back in Nazareth, the village was alive with excitement and anticipation. The news of Joseph and Mary's return and their imminent marriage spread through the town like wildfire. They all seemed to know that Mary was present at the miraculous birth of Elizabeth and Zachariah's baby. This made her a celebrity of sorts as well

Their local family and friends gathered to celebrate their blessed union. Hannah, Rachel, Isaac, Esther and Levi, as well as Cleopas, Mary and others from Joseph's family were all there to help celebrate Mary and Joseph's love for one another. Music filled the air, and echoed through the town square.

As the sun began to set, Joseph and Mary stood before their family and friends, surrounded by the glow of love and happiness. They had asked Isaac to officiate the ceremony, invoking prayers and blessings upon the couple.

The exchange of vows was a moment of profound significance. Joseph looked into Mary's eyes, his voice filled with love and devotion, as he promised to cherish and protect her, to walk by her side through all of life's joys and trials.

Mary's voice trembled with emotion as she spoke her vows, her heart overflowing with love and gratitude for the man before her. She pledged to stand by him, to support and love him as they embarked on this sacred journey together.

As the elder pronounced them husband and wife, the family erupted in cheers and applause. Tears of joy streamed down Mary's cheeks, and Joseph beamed with pride. Their union was not only a celebration of their love but a testament to God's divine plan.

As the days passed after the joyful marriage celebration, Joseph and Mary prepared for their journey to Bethlehem. The Roman census required them to travel to Joseph's ancestral home, which was no small undertaking.

The village elders and friends came together to offer their support and blessings. They provided food, water, and essential supplies for the journey. Mary's parents embraced her tightly, praying for her safety and the well-being of the unborn child.

With hearts full of love and faith, Joseph and Mary bid farewell to their families and the village they held dear. The road ahead was long and uncertain, but they knew that God's hand was guiding their path.

Joseph placed Mary carefully on the donkey and they set off on their journey to Bethlehem, embracing the adventure and the divine purpose that lay ahead.

The 4 day minimum journey to Bethlehem was not without challenges. The roads were crowded with other travelers heading to register for the census, and finding any accommodation was no easy task. As days passed, Mary grew weary, and Joseph's concern deepened. He sought every opportunity to provide comfort and care for her, even as he faced his own uncertainties.

At times, they faced harsh weather and long stretches of travel with no water. Yet, Mary's unwavering faith and Joseph's steadfast dedication to her kept them moving forward. One evening, as the sun began to set, Joseph and Mary found themselves in the outskirts of Bethlehem. The journey had been taxing, and they were both fatigued. They had been turned away from several inns that were filled to capacity with travelers.

Feeling disheartened, Joseph looked at Mary with concern. "I am sorry, my love," he said, "I did not anticipate such difficulties in finding a place to rest."

Mary smiled reassuringly, her unwavering faith shining in her eyes. "Fear not, Joseph," she said, "God will provide."

As they continued their search, their steps led them to a humble inn on the outskirts of Bethlehem. Joseph knocked on the door, and a kind innkeeper greeted them. "I have no room left in the inn," he said, "but you are welcome to seek shelter in the stable."

Grateful for any respite, Joseph led Mary inside. He spread a soft blanket on the straw-covered floor and made a makeshift bed for her.

In the dim light of the stable, Mary felt a sense of peace wash over her. She knew that God's hand was guiding them, and that this unexpected setting was part of His divine plan. She kept thinking back of the studies she, Hannah and Rachel had about how much the Messiah would have to suffer. She prayed the suffering she had to endure on this journey could somehow take away from the suffering He would have to endure, that it would be worth it.

As the stars twinkled in the night sky, Joseph held Mary close, offering comfort and warmth. He knew that they were part of something extraordinary, and he marveled at the depth of Mary's faith and strength.

In the stillness of that holy night, Mary gave birth to her son, Jesus. The cries of the newborn filled the stable, and Joseph's heart swelled with overwhelming love and gratitude. Wrapping the baby in swaddling clothes, Mary cradled her newborn in her arms. Tears of joy streamed down her cheeks as she looked at her precious child, the long-awaited Savior of the world.

Joseph knelt beside her, his heart brimming with awe. "He is here," he whispered, his voice trembling with emotion. "Our son, the Son of God."

The shepherds in the nearby fields received a heavenly visitation, as an angel appeared to them, proclaiming the birth of the Savior. Filled with awe and joy, they hurried to the stable under the bright star to witness the divine miracle.

As the world rejoiced, Mary and Joseph held each other close, knowing that their love had been chosen to play a crucial role in God's grand design. In the midst of the bustling town, they found solace in the knowledge that their journey was guided by divine providence.

With hearts full of love and devotion, they gazed at their newborn son, their hearts overflowing with gratitude for the miracles that had unfolded in their lives.

As the stars shone bright above Bethlehem, Mary, Joseph, and the newborn Jesus basked in the glow of divine love, knowing that they were embarking on a journey that would change the course of human history. The innkeeper and his wife came out with warm and dry blankets and buckets filled with both warm and cold water to help them freshen up. They said the inn would be full for several weeks, but they could stay there as long as they would like.

As the days passed, the humble stable in Bethlehem became a place of wonder and worship. People from all walks of life visited to catch a glimpse of the infant Savior, and their hearts were touched by the radiance of God's love.

Joseph and Mary were visited by wise men from distant lands, who had followed a wondrous star to pay homage to the newborn King. They presented gifts of gold, frankincense, and myrrh, symbolic of the reverence they held for the divine child. As they left, they told Joseph that they had passed by the king's palace and he wanted them to stop on their way home to tell him precisely where the baby king was found. They said that they would return home a different way, but suggested Mary and Joseph take the baby and hide from Herod.

Amidst the joy and celebration and this new worry of Herod, Mary and Joseph still found comfort in their love for one another and in the knowledge that they were chosen to be part of God's divine plan. Their hearts overflowed with gratitude for the love that bound their family together and would keep them safe.

The next morning, being the fortieth day after Jesus' birth, Mary and Joseph brought the baby Jesus to the Temple in Jerusalem to fulfill the Jewish law, which required that the firstborn male child be presented to the Lord and redeemed with an offering, as prescribed in the story of Exodus. This was very risky as King Herod was ruling over Judea, and his palace was located in Jerusalem, the political and administrative center of the region.

But they also knew every day, a larger crowd came to see the baby Savior of the Jews, so staying in Bethlehem was just as dangerous.

After the Presentation of Jesus in the Temple, Mary and Joseph were filled with gratitude and awe as they made their way through the bustling streets of Jerusalem. Their hearts were brimming with the significance of the moment, knowing that their precious son had been consecrated to the Lord but recognizing they had to leave Jerusalem before anyone spotted them and recognized them.

As they walked, they spotted an elderly couple, Simeon and his wife, Anna, who were known for their devout faith and wisdom. Simeon had been eagerly awaiting the arrival of the promised Messiah, and he had received a divine revelation that he would not die before laying eyes upon the Savior.

Mary and Joseph felt drawn to this couple, sensing that there was a divine connection between them. As they approached, Simeon's eyes met Mary's, and he felt a surge of joy and recognition in his heart. He knew that the child in her arms was the long-awaited Messiah.

"Peace be with you," Simeon greeted them, his voice filled with reverence and love. "This child is destined to bring salvation to many and to be a light to the Gentiles."

Tears welled up in Mary's eyes as she listened to Simeon's prophetic words. She held Jesus closer, feeling the weight of the divine destiny he carried. Joseph stood by her side, his heart overflowing with gratitude for the honor bestowed upon them.

Simeon reached out to hold the child in his arms, and a sense of peace washed over him. He had waited his whole life for this moment, and now, he felt a profound sense of fulfillment and contentment.

"I have seen the salvation of our God," Simeon proclaimed, his voice ringing with conviction. "This child is a sign of God's love and mercy for all humanity."

Mary and Joseph exchanged glances, their hearts filled with wonder at the divine confirmation they had received through Simeon's words. They continued to see signs that they were part of a grand plan, entrusted with the care of the Savior of the world.

As they continued to converse with Simeon and Anna, they realized that the elderly couple had been praying for the coming of the Messiah for many years. Their faith and devotion touched Mary and Joseph deeply, inspiring them to embrace their role as parents of the chosen one with even greater resolve.

Simeon blessed God and spoke directly to Mary: "Behold, this child is appointed for the fall and rising of many in Israel, and for a sign that is opposed and a sword will pierce through your own soul also, so that thoughts from many hearts may be revealed."

Mary knew, that in this prophecy, Simeon was foretelling Jesus' life and mission will have a significant impact on many people. He will bring both salvation and judgment to Israel. That many will be uplifted and drawn closer to God by His teachings and miracles, while others will reject and oppose him.

She also knew the profound sorrow and pain that she will endure as a result of her son's mission. The phrase "a sword will pierce through your own soul also" alludes to the anguish and grief she will experience as she witnesses the suffering and death of Jesus on the cross.

This prophecy underscores the dual nature of Jesus' mission as both a source of salvation and a point of division. It highlights the profound sacrifice that Mary will make as the mother of the Savior, even as she experiences immense joy and pride in her role.

Mary and Joseph's hearts pounded with urgency and fear as they swiftly left Jerusalem behind, journeying southwest toward Egypt, seeking safety away from Herod's malevolent grasp. The shadows of Herod's evil deeds loomed large in their minds, but they clung to hope, knowing that their baby boy was destined to wield a profound influence on people's lives.

As they traveled, Joseph and Mary shared whispered conversations, their voices filled with both determination and awe. They marveled at the divine purpose entrusted to their child, recognizing the threat this posed to the forces of darkness.

"The evil one must be trembling in fear," Joseph said, his eyes fixed on the road ahead. "Our son will lead people to follow Him, not to descend into the dark abyss satan inhabits."

Mary's heart swelled with pride and love for her son, even as tears welled in her eyes, knowing the trials he would face. "Indeed," she replied, her voice unwavering, "Our son Jesus will shine like a beacon of hope, dispelling darkness and guiding souls toward the path of light and love."

Their resolve strengthened with every step, for they understood the magnitude of their mission as protectors of the divine gift entrusted to them. They knew that in safeguarding Jesus, they were shielding the world from the clutches of evil.

As they journeyed onward, they were comforted by a sense of divine presence, guiding and shielding them from serious harm, at least until His mission was completed. They knew that the path would not be easy, but they also knew that the light of their son's love and teachings would illuminate the hearts of many, leading them out of the shadows and into the embrace of God's grace.

In their hearts, Mary and Joseph carried the weight of the world's salvation, fully aware of the sacrifices they would have to make. They knew that they were not only protecting their son but safeguarding a future of hope and redemption for all humanity.

With each passing mile, they drew closer to Egypt, a land of refuge and safety. Their faith in God's providence carried them through the darkest moments, for they knew that the divine hand was guiding their steps and shaping the destiny of their beloved son.

As they journeyed, they clung to the certainty that their little Jesus would grow up to fulfill his divine purpose, transforming lives and leading countless souls toward the path of righteousness. In their trust and love, they found the strength to face whatever trials lay ahead, knowing that their baby boy would be a beacon of light and hope in a world yearning for salvation.

And so, Mary and Joseph pressed on, their hearts ablaze with love, courage, and hope. The weight of their mission was great, but the power of divine love, shining through their precious child, would be even greater. They embraced their role as guardians of the Savior, determined to shield him from harm, for they knew that his light would dispel darkness and lead humanity back into the loving arms of God.

Once they arrived safely in Alexandria, they gave praise to God for providing that safe passage and asked for safety upon their families in Nazareth. They would seek out a reliable northern traveler who could pass on a message to their friends and family that they were safe in Egypt and would return to Nazareth as soon as they could do so safely.

In the meantime, they would find employment for Joseph and a safe place to live, spending their free time looking into the eyes of their newborn son, knowing that his destiny was entwined with that of humanity. He was the long-awaited Messiah, the Savior of the world, and his life would be marked by both joy and sacrifice.

In the quiet moments of the night, Mary would cradle Jesus in her arms and share stories of the angel's visit, the prophecies, and the profound love that surrounded his miraculous birth.

She would tell him of the faith and courage that Joseph had displayed, his unwavering support and love that had carried them through the challenges of their journey.

And as Mary held her precious son close, she knew that their family's love was an enduring testament to the boundless love of God, who had chosen them to play a pivotal role in the salvation of humanity.

A Hard Lesson for All

Once the news of Herod's demise reached Egypt, Mary, Joseph, and young Jesus knew that the time had come to return to their homeland, Nazareth. The journey was long and arduous, but they traveled with a renewed sense of purpose and gratitude, knowing that God's protective hand had guided them through the perils of Herod's tyranny.

As they made their way back to Nazareth, Mary and Joseph remained vigilant, ever aware of the lurking threat that the evil one posed. They knew that the fallen angel would stop at nothing to derail God's divine plan, and they resolved to shield Jesus from harm with unwavering vigilance and love.

Upon their safe return to Nazareth, Mary and Joseph settled into their quiet life, cherishing the moments they spent with their growing son. As Jesus matured, his wisdom and understanding surpassed his tender age, leaving those around him in awe of his divine nature.

Being back in Nazareth, the family resumed the beautiful tradition of making an annual pilgrimage to Jerusalem for the Passover feast. This journey not only reaffirmed their faith in God but also served as a reminder of the divine mission that rested on young Jesus' shoulders.

Every year, they traveled to Jerusalem with a sense of both anticipation and trepidation. They knew that the evil one would seize any opportunity to strike, and they remained on high alert, watching over Jesus with the love and protection that only devoted parents could provide.

On one fateful pilgrimage, as they traveled back to Nazareth after the Passover celebrations, a feeling of unease gripped Mary's heart. She scanned the crowd, searching for her beloved son, but he was nowhere to be found. Panic washed over her, and she turned to Joseph, her eyes filled with tears.

"We've lost him," she whispered, her voice trembling with fear. "The evil one must have found a way to snatch him away from us."

Joseph's heart sank, but he refused to give in to despair. Together, they retraced their steps, scouring the streets of Jerusalem for any sign of Jesus. Their love for their son was a fierce flame that burned bright, fending off the darkness that threatened to consume them.

Three days passed, each moment heavy with worry and anguish. Then, in the Temple, they found him, sitting among the teachers, listening intently and asking profound questions that left the wise men astonished.

Relief washed over Mary and Joseph as they approached their son, embracing him tightly. Yet, their worry lingered, and Mary questioned Jesus with a mixture of relief and reproach, "Son, why have you treated us so? Your father and I have been anxiously searching for you."

Jesus smiled gently, his eyes brimming with love and understanding. "Why were you searching for me?" he replied. "Did you not know that I must be in my Father's house?"

The revelation of Jesus' profound awareness of his divine mission left Mary and Joseph both amazed and humbled. In that moment, they understood that their son was not only their child but the Savior of all humanity, destined to fulfill God's grand design. There was so much to learn from this event.

The experience in the temple taught Mary the importance of surrendering her worries and fears to God. Despite her initial panic and anxiety when Jesus went missing, Mary eventually found solace in knowing that Jesus was safe in his Father's house. She learned to trust in God's divine plan and to let go of the need for control. This experience deepened her understanding of her role as the mother of the Savior and strengthened her faith in God's guidance and protection.

Joseph, too, learned the power of faith and patience. As a protective father, he had felt immense responsibility for the safety of his family, especially Jesus. However, the temple incident taught him to have faith in God's providence and to remain steadfast even in moments of uncertainty. He learned that God's plans often unfold in mysterious ways, and his role as a guardian was not to control every outcome but to trust in God's wisdom and love.

For young Jesus, the experience in the temple was a moment of profound self-awareness and understanding of his divine identity. It reinforced his awareness of his unique relationship with God as the Son of the Father. He learned the importance of fulfilling his divine mission, sharing God's love and teachings with all people, even at a young age. This experience also deepened his compassion and empathy for those who seek the truth and the light, guiding them away from darkness and sin.

Collectively, the Holy Family learned the value of open communication and mutual support. As they reunited in the temple, they shared their fears, joys, and revelations, strengthening their bond as a family chosen to play an extraordinary role in God's plan for salvation.

The experience in the temple also affirmed the significance of Jesus' mission, not only for his earthly family but for all of humanity. It served as a poignant reminder that Jesus was not just an ordinary child but the Messiah, destined to bring light and redemption to the world.

Ultimately, the episode in the temple deepened Mary, Joseph, and Jesus' trust in God's divine guidance and affirmed their commitment to their unique roles in God's plan. It was a moment of spiritual growth and realization that shaped their understanding of their individual identities and their collective purpose as a family chosen to be part of the most significant story in human history.

As they made their way back to Nazareth, their hearts were filled with awe and wonder at the unfolding mystery of God's plan. Jesus, with his boundless love and wisdom, knew the maneuverings of the evil one and was already steps ahead, sharing the message of God's love and mercy with the temple leaders, even for sinners who would choose repentance over the darkness.

In the years that followed, Mary and Joseph continued to watch over their son with love and devotion, knowing that he was the light that would dispel the shadows of the evil one's designs. They stood as pillars of strength, knowing that God's divine protection would guide their every step, and that Jesus' love and teachings would lead humanity back to the path of righteousness.

As the years passed and Jesus' earthly ministry unfolded, Mary and Joseph embraced their roles with unwavering faith, knowing that they were guardians of God's greatest gift to humanity. They took comfort in the knowledge that their son was not just their salvation but the salvation of the world.

Cana

In the quiet town of Nazareth, the passing of time brought new chapters to the lives of Mary, Joseph, and Jesus. As Jesus approached his thirties, the veil of time began to cast shadows on Joseph's earthly journey. The tender bond that Jesus shared with Joseph was profound and unique. Joseph had been his earthly father, his mentor, and a guiding light throughout his upbringing.

Mary, wise and attuned to the rhythms of God's plan, saw the impact of Joseph's impending death on Jesus. She observed the struggle within him – the desire to keep Joseph alive to continue supporting and protecting her, yet also yearning for him to receive the heavenly reward he so rightfully deserved. Jesus, knowing the Father's divine plan, grappled with the delicate balance between his human love for Joseph and the larger purpose of salvation.

As Joseph's final days approached, he and Jesus shared precious moments of wisdom, love, and guidance. In Joseph's peaceful passing, Jesus witnessed the fulfillment of his earthly father's role in God's redemptive plan. His heart ached with loss, yet he understood the eternal significance of Joseph's legacy.

Amid the weight of grief, Jesus began his public ministry. At the wedding feast in Cana, he stood on the precipice of revealing his divine nature to the world. Mary, always attuned to his heart, saw the significance of this moment. With the gentle wisdom of a mother who knows her child's destiny, she approached Jesus with the simple plea, "They have no more wine."

In her voice, Jesus heard the echoes of his mother's "yes" to the angel's message, and he knew that she was aware of the challenges he would face. In his human heart, he also sensed her understanding of the burdens he would bear, physically, emotionally, and spiritually. With a smile of both love and reverence, he answered her, "Woman, what does this have to do with me? My hour has not yet come."

Mary, undeterred, turned to the servants and said, "Do whatever he tells you." In these words, she asserted her role as the mother of God Incarnate, demonstrating her trust in his divine wisdom and authority. She knew that Jesus practiced the commandment to honor one's father and mother, and in honoring her, he would exemplify this divine virtue.

With a quiet command, Jesus directed the servants to fill the jars with water, and miraculously, the water turned into wine – the finest wine that the wedding guests had ever tasted. In this first recorded miracle, Jesus not only validated his divine authority but also laid the groundwork for a deep spiritual truth. By allowing Mary's intercession, he revealed that she had a unique role in heaven's court, advocating for those who sincerely sought her help.

As the story of the wedding at Cana spread, people marveled at Jesus' power, and Mary's insight into his divinity. Her simple yet profound words, "Do whatever he tells you," resonated with hearts seeking guidance. Jesus rewarded her trust and faithfulness, knowing that her maternal heart was forever intertwined with his mission.

In this miracle, Jesus also showcased his profound compassion. Just as he transformed water into wine, he would transform sorrow into joy, sin into redemption, and despair into hope. The miracle spoke of his divine power, but also of his unwavering love for humanity.

In the midst of the celebration, as the wine flowed and laughter filled the air, Mary and Jesus shared a knowing glance. It was a silent acknowledgment of the bond they shared, of the challenges they would face together, and of the world-transforming journey that lay ahead.

And so, the story of the wedding at Cana became a testament to the unity of mother and Son, of divine compassion, and of the infinite power of love to transform lives and hearts.

Parables Tell Multiple Stories

More than three decades had slipped by since the moment Mary, with unwavering resolve, responded to the call of the Lord through the angel Gabriel. However, every passing day served as a poignant reminder of the profound implications etched upon her heart. She knew, as intimately as the verses of scripture she had committed to memory, that her son would bear a tremendous burden of pain and suffering. The intricacies of the prophecy remained veiled, the details shrouded in uncertainty. Yet, amidst the uncertainty, a steadfast conviction took root within her: that despite the agonies He would face, ultimate victory would grace her son's journey.

Mary's acceptance of her role as the Mother of Christ wasn't a decision made lightly. It was an acceptance rooted in her unwavering faith and her intimate connection with God's divine plan. She knew that her son's journey would be one of trials and tribulations, but it was a journey she embraced with love and devotion.

Within the corridors of her mind, Mary retraced the solemn path of Lucifer's fall from grace. The archangel's irreversible decision to forsake heaven had eternally sealed his fate. Mary understood that his descent, once adorned with angelic splendor, had been marred by greed and the desire to wield authority. Yet, even in his error, Lucifer's malicious mission on Earth remained a relentless pursuit, to ensnare souls into the abyss of eternal suffering. He had chosen the path of war against the divine, a war that could inflict but a fleeting ache upon God's heart when one of His lost sheep strayed further into darkness.

As Mary's understanding deepened, so did her appreciation of God's design of Free Will and the role of atonement. The past three decades had seen her, Joseph, and Jesus shoulder their own shares of hardships, a part of the grand tapestry of God the Father's master plan. With each passing trial, Mary had grappled with the significance of her son's mission and the suffering He would endure. Yet, even as she contemplated these mysteries, she was on the brink of a revelation that would transform her perception of the path laid before them.

In the tranquil embrace of Nazareth, Mary's heart was a repository of wisdom that transcended human understanding. As Jesus embarked on his public ministry, his parables resonated with both promise and foreboding. For within their layers of meaning, Mary discerned not only the seeds of hope but also the looming specter of suffering that would cast its shadow over their lives.

One warm afternoon, under the gentle shade of the olive trees, Jesus sat surrounded by his disciples and a crowd eager to hear his teachings. Mary, ever watchful and filled with a mother's intuition, listened attentively as her son wove stories that held layers of profound meaning.

As Jesus unveiled the Parable of the Sower, Mary recognized the depth of his words. The seeds, cast upon various types of soil, mirrored the reception of his message. With a heavy heart, she understood that the Kingdom of God, while bringing transformation, would encounter resistance and trials. The path to establishing this kingdom, she knew, might involve the very hardships that weighed on her soul.

The Parable of the Good Samaritan resonated deeply within Mary's heart. She saw her son's reflection in the compassionate Samaritan, one who would reach out to heal the broken and offer solace to the wounded. Yet, as a mother, she also glimpsed the potential for pain in her son's path. Just as the Samaritan faced danger to care for a stranger, she knew that Jesus's love would lead him to suffering for the sake of others.

With the Parable of the Prodigal Son, Mary felt the ache of recognition. The father's open arms, forgiving and welcoming, mirrored the essence of her son's mission. She comprehended that his journey would involve confronting humanity's brokenness, mending hearts shattered by sin. Yet, her mother's heart couldn't help but grimace at the knowledge that like the parable, the brother's anger with not only his brother, but also the father could be foretelling anger and retaliation against Jesus.

As the sun lowered below the horizon, Mary retreated to the quiet of her home. Amidst the soft candlelight, she pondered the profound truths embedded in her son's parables. The prophetic whispers of the Torah resonated within her, guiding her understanding. She knew that the Messiah's role would encompass both redemption and sacrifice, the building of a new kingdom intertwined with the suffering of an old world.

A New Radiance

In the serene hills of Nazareth, a new day dawned and Mary's heart remained steadfast in its understanding of her son's divine mission. The air was filled with a gentle breeze as she reflected on the journey that lay ahead for Jesus. As he approached the pinnacle of his ministry, Mary's devotion deepened, and her acceptance of the role of Mother of Christ became even more resolute.

One day, as the sun bathed the landscape in a warm embrace, Mary heard whispers of a transformative event that had taken place in her son's life. It was the Transfiguration – a moment when Jesus's earthly form was illuminated by a heavenly radiance. As John's description of the event reached her ears, her heart quickened with anticipation.

Guided by a quiet intuition, Mary made her way to a solitary place to pray. Beneath the shade of an ancient olive tree, she closed her eyes, and in the depths of her contemplation, she sensed the presence of God's glory. She envisioned her son, his face bathed in celestial light, his divinity shining through the veil of his humanity.

In her heart, Mary recognized the profound significance of this event. The radiant transformation she had heard about was a glimpse into the heavenly realm that was both her son's origin and destination. She knew the divine brilliance would be contrasted with the suffering he would endure, and her mother's heart quivered with the wicked thoughts of what lay ahead.

As she pondered the vision of the Transfiguration, Mary's gaze shifted to the horizon. Her son's path, illuminated by both heavenly glory and earthly pain, became clearer to her. She knew that the radiance of his divine nature was not a contradiction to his impending suffering, but rather a confirmation of his divine identity, even if only witnessed by Peter, James and John.

With this understanding, Mary's resolve deepened. She recognized that her acceptance of her role as Mother of Christ was a commitment to accompany him on his journey – a journey that would be marked by both triumph and tribulation. The imagined vision of the Transfiguration became a source of strength for her, a reminder that the suffering her son would face was not without purpose.

With a heart filled with love and unwavering faith, Mary continued to stand by her son's side as he navigated the challenges of his ministry. Her acceptance of the Messiah's mission, complete with the knowledge of his future suffering, would temper her pain through the trials they would face together.

The mental image of the Transfiguration, with its heavenly radiance and earthly contrasts, became a guiding light for Mary. It fortified her resolve to support her son through his trials, to hold him close in the face of adversity, and to embrace her role in God's divine plan. In that moment of divine revelation, Mary's heart beat in harmony with the eternal rhythm of love, sacrifice, and redemption that would define her son's remaining earthly journey – a journey that would ultimately transform the world.

The Sacrificial Lamb

In the quiet of the night of the Passover Supper, Mary's heart was a tapestry woven with threads of love and understanding. As the moon's glow bathed Jerusalem in a silvery light, she recalled the journey that she and her son, Jesus, had embarked upon. Her acceptance of her role as Mother of Christ had always been entwined with the knowledge of his mission, a mission that would demand both triumph and tribulation.

From across the Kidron Valley, she heard whispers of her son's anguished prayers, his plea for the cup of suffering to pass from him, and her mother's heart ached.

Guided by an innate understanding of the Scriptures from the Torah, Mary drew parallels between Jesus's agony in Gethsemane in which she heard on this new silent night and the prophetic suffering of the Messiah. In the sacred texts, she had encountered passages that spoke of the Messiah's affliction, his role as a Suffering Servant who would bear the weight of the world's sin.

She knew that the burden he carried, the weight of the world's sin, was immense and overwhelming. It was a burden that extended beyond the physical realm, reaching into the depths of the human experience. She knew that there had been and would be many who rejected Jesus and His Teachings, yet because of His message of love for all, He would suffer for them and their sins as well.

In the stillness of her contemplation, Mary imagined herself standing beside her son in the garden, their souls united in their shared purpose. She saw the tears that mingled with his prayers, the unspoken anguish etched upon his face. And though her heart ached, she recognized the necessity of his suffering for the redemption of humanity.

This event and the events over the next day would be like a refining fire, deepened her compassion and commitment to being his mother. It strengthened the resolve she had carried since Gabriel's announcement – a resolve that had taken into account the knowledge of her son's divine destiny. Her love for him was unwavering, and her understanding of his mission fortified her acceptance of the pain he would endure.

In the midst of the night's silence, Mary held close to her heart the truth that had guided her journey from the beginning: the Messiah's path would be one of sacrifice, and her role as Mother of Christ encompassed both joy and sorrow. Through the trials that lay immediately ahead, she found solace in the profound understanding that his suffering was not in vain. It was a part of God's divine plan – a plan that would ultimately lead to the redemption of humanity.

And so, in the midst of her own pains and fears, Mary drew strength from the knowledge that her son's suffering was a pivotal moment in the tapestry of salvation. Her acceptance of her role as Mother of Christ was unwavering, rooted in love, faith, and an understanding that his pain would lead to the ultimate victory of love over darkness, of redemption over sin, but the next hours would reflect Simeon's prophecy of a sword piercing her heart, and she could feel it already.

On the hill of Golgotha, a scene of anguish unfolded under the unforgiving sun. Mary stood at the foot of the cross, her heart torn between love and sorrow, her soul anchored to the fulfillment of a divine plan. As she watched her son, Jesus, endure the excruciating torment of crucifixion, she found herself grappling with a mixture of emotions – a mother's agony intertwined with the understanding of a prophetic purpose.

In the midst of the crowd's mournful wails, Mary's gaze never wavered from her son. Her hands clenched in fists at her sides, her eyes welled with tears that mirrored the pain etched on Jesus's face. As a devout Jew, Mary carried within her the sacred teachings of the Torah, the echoes of the prophetic words that had foretold the Messiah's suffering.

She recalled the words of Isaiah, the prophecies of the suffering Servant who would bear the iniquities of many, who would be despised and afflicted. These verses had been woven into her understanding of the Messiah's role since her youth. As she stood at the foot of the cross, she recognized the fulfillment of these prophecies in her own beloved son.

With each labored breath he took, each drop of blood that fell to the ground, Jesus was confirming the ancient words spoken by the prophets. The weight of his sacrifice was not lost on Mary; it was etched into the depths of her soul. She understood that his suffering was not merely physical, but a profound spiritual ordeal that carried the sins of humanity. His blood, from the most perfect, unblemished Lamb of God, poured out on Her Mantle that the angel of death would never come near her, but pass on to others.

Amidst the agony of the moment, Mary's heart held firm to the knowledge that her acceptance of her role as Mother of Christ had taken into account this very suffering. She knew that the path of the Messiah, as foretold by the prophets, would involve great pain and trials. As a mother, she had embraced this reality, understanding that his mission was not one of comfort and ease, but of redemption and sacrifice. Nonetheless, He was her son, and the pain of His suffering pained her to her core.

As the sky darkened and the world seemed to hold its breath, Mary's gaze remained fixed on her son's anguished form. The prophetic threads that had woven through her life were now merging with the present moment. She understood that his suffering was not in vain, that his sacrifice was the cornerstone of God's divine plan for salvation.

With a heart that both mourned and rejoiced, Mary stood as a witness to the fulfillment of prophecy. She understood that her son's pain was a testament to his unwavering love for humanity, a love that surpassed the boundaries of time and space. Through her tears, she held fast to the understanding that his suffering was a necessary part of the redemption story, a story that would bring light out of darkness, life out of death.

As the world trembled and the weight of the moment hung heavy in the air, Mary's acceptance of her role as Mother of Christ was unwavering. With a mother's love and a profound faith, she embraced the anguish and sacrifice, knowing that her son's suffering would pave the way for a new dawn of hope, a salvation that would transcend the bounds of earthly pain.

Dull with emotional pain, she grasped the hand of John who stood by her through the greatest suffering ever. She turned to him and said, "Jesus proclaimed His mission was finished. He has conquered sin with His suffering and death. But soon, He will show us that He will conquer not only sin, but will conquer death as well! We must remain steadfast as our mission has just begun!"

In the quiet dawn of the third day, a radiant light pierced the darkness, illuminating the world with a glimmer of divine promise. Mary, her heart still heavy from the agony of witnessing her son's crucifixion, was excited to hear reports from those first to approach the tomb. They ran back proclaiming that As they drew near, their eyes widened in awe, for before them lay an empty tomb, its stone rolled away. The Resurrection had unfolded, a testament to the victory over death.

A mixture of excitement and hope stirred within Mary's heart. The weight of the events leading to the crucifixion still clung to her soul, yet the reports before her held the promise of a new beginning.

She remembered the prophecies, the teachings of the Torah that spoke of the Messiah's triumph over death. As a devout Jew, these words resonated deep within her, intertwined with her understanding of God's ultimate plan.

The Resurrection had filled Mary with both awe and hope. She recognized that the Messiah's suffering wasn't the end, but a necessary step toward victory over death. The tears she had shed at the foot of the cross were now transformed to tears of wonder and joy. Her mother's heart, so acquainted with both pain and love, felt the surge of divine power that had shattered the chains of mortality and sin.

As the morning sun cast its golden rays upon the landscape, Mary's heart was filled with a profound sense of peace. The Resurrection was a proclamation that the Messiah's journey, marked by suffering and sacrifice, had led to a victory beyond measure. Her acceptance of her role as Mother of Christ had led her to this moment of transformation, a moment that radiated with the light of eternity.

With renewed faith, Mary embraced the reality that her son's resurrection was not only a fulfillment of prophecy but also a testament to the unending love and mercy of God the Father. Through her tears of joy, she glimpsed the eternal tapestry of God's plan, where suffering was not the end, but a means to an even greater purpose.

With a heart that held both the memory of pain and the promise of glory, Mary stood as a witness to the Resurrection. Her acceptance of her role as Mother of Christ had led her to this pivotal moment in history – a moment that affirmed the profound truth that suffering, though agonizing, was transformed into victory through the love of a God who had conquered death itself.

Looking Up and Forward

Weeks later, on a hilltop overlooking Jerusalem, the air was charged with a sense of anticipation. Mary stood among the disciples, her eyes fixed on her son, Jesus, as he spoke his final words to them. The time had come for his Ascension, a moment that would fill her heart with a mixture of emotions – awe, pride, and a bittersweet sense of letting go.

As Jesus began to ascend, his form gradually disappearing into the heavens, Mary's heart swelled with both joy and sorrow. Her journey with her son had been marked by moments of unimaginable pain and boundless love. From the manger to the cross, she had walked beside him, holding in her heart the knowledge that his role as Messiah would involve great suffering.

The Ascension stirred Mary's heart with bittersweet emotions. As Jesus returned to heaven, she might have contemplated his continued work as the exalted Messiah. She had witnessed the divine radiance that had shone through him, the same radiance that had transformed her understanding of his mission. Now, as he ascended, she knew that his role was far from over – he was returning to the Father, to continue his work in the spiritual realm. Her heart swelled with a sense of pride as she saw her son, the Son of God, take his place at the right hand of the Father.

In the midst of the disciples' awe and wonder, Mary's gaze held a deep understanding. Her acceptance of her role as Mother of Christ had taken into account the knowledge that his mission would involve not only earthly suffering but also divine purpose. As he ascended, she held fast to the truth that his suffering had not been in vain, that his sacrifice had paved the way for a new era of redemption and grace.

As the disciples continued to gaze upward, Mary's heart was a mosaic of emotions. She understood that the Ascension was a moment of transformation, a moment that affirmed her faith in God's ultimate plan. Her acceptance of her role as Mother of Christ had led her to this pivotal juncture, a juncture where earthly suffering intersected with heavenly purpose.

With a mother's love that transcended time and space, Mary watched as her son disappeared from sight. Her heart was filled with gratitude for the privilege of being his mother, for witnessing his life, death, and resurrection. And as she stood there, her faith unwavering, she knew that the journey she had embarked upon was far from over. Her son's legacy, his teachings, his love – they would continue to echo through the ages, a testament to the enduring power of the Messiah's sacrifice.

The Advocate

In the upper room, a sense of anticipation hung in the air like a gathering storm. Mary was among the disciples who had gathered, their hearts beating in unison as they waited for the promised outpouring of the Holy Spirit. The memory of her son, Jesus, was alive within her, his teachings, his love, and his ultimate sacrifice etched into her very being. As the disciples prayed fervently, Mary's gaze held a depth of understanding born from years of witnessing her son's journey.

When the rushing wind and tongues of fire filled the room, Mary's heart quickened with a mixture of awe and recognition. The event of Pentecost was unfolding before her eyes, a testament to the fulfillment of Jesus's promise to be with them always. The Advocate, Holy Spirit, descended upon the disciples, igniting their hearts with divine fire and filling them with a newfound courage and boldness.

For Mary, this moment held profound significance. She knew that her acceptance of her role as Mother of Christ had encompassed the understanding that his mission would involve great suffering and ultimate triumph. Now, as she witnessed the disciples empowered by the same Holy Spirit, she saw the continuation of her son's work, a work that would transcend time and space.

The event of Pentecost reminded Mary of the promise Jesus had made to his disciples – that he would send the Comforter, the Advocate, to guide and strengthen them. She recognized the profound connection between her son's sacrifice and the empowerment of the early Church. The Holy Spirit was the tangible manifestation of God's presence, sustaining and guiding the disciples as they spread the message of love and redemption.

As the disciples spoke in languages they had not known before, Mary's heart swelled with a sense of purpose. She saw the early Church coming to life, infused with the same Spirit that had guided her son throughout his ministry. Amid the tumultuous times and challenges they would face, the Holy Spirit would be their anchor, their source of courage, and their constant guide.

In the midst of the disciples' exultation, Mary's gaze held a quiet strength. She understood that the journey she had embarked upon, marked by the acceptance of her role as Mother of Christ, had led to this transformative moment. The suffering she had witnessed, the trials she had endured, were now part of a tapestry that was being woven anew through the power of the Holy Spirit.

With a heart that had held both the weight of sorrow and the promise of joy, Mary stood as a witness to Pentecost. Her faith in God's plan was unwavering, her acceptance of her son's mission resolute. As the disciples stepped out into the world, emboldened by the Spirit, Mary's heart was filled with hope. The suffering of the past was now the foundation upon which the early Church would be built, and the promise of redemption would echo through the ages.

Amidst these unfolding events, Mary's comprehension of the Messiah's destined suffering would have grown deeper, woven with threads of insight and revelation. The prophecies engraved upon her heart from the teachings of the Torah, combined with her intimate experiences of Jesus's life, teachings, and miraculous deeds, merged to create a rich tapestry of unwavering faith and profound understanding.

With each step of her journey beside her son, Mary's understanding evolved. The seeds of prophecy found fertile ground in the reality of Jesus's ministry, passion, crucifixion, and triumphant resurrection. Her acceptance of her unique role as the mother of the Messiah became not only a steadfast commitment but a fortress of conviction, strengthened by her profound comprehension of the divine orchestration at play and her resolute reliance on God's providential care.

Also by John H Brennan

Thru The First Disciple's Eyes
Thru the First Disciple's Eyes
Through the Eyes of the Disciple Jesus Loved
Through the Eyes of Cleopas

Standalone
Advice From Above
The Rosary Revealed
Yes, I Knew!

About the Author

John is a cradle Catholic, the middle child of five, who grew up in upstate New York. Vatican Two saved him from learning Latin the year he trained to be an Altar Server. He attended Catholic School until High School when he transitioned to public school. He received two associates degrees from the local Community College, then started a job in a fortune 500 company as a draftsman. He had met the woman of his dreams and they had the first of their children 9 months after they were married. Six months later, the three headed off to the State University of New York at Buffalo where John studied Mechanical Engineering. By the time John graduated with his BS in Mechanical Engineering, they had their second son and headed back to his hometown to continue his 40 year career and have a third son and finally his daughter. He and his wife now have a son in law, a daughter in law and six beautiful grandchildren. Several events led him to deepen his faith – joining a Catholic Men's Bible Study; attending several Catholic Men's Conferences; attending a Catholic Men's Emmaus Retreat as well as being on several Emmaus Retreat Teams (including giving witness talks); attending daily Mass; Praying the Holy Rosary daily and being an Extraordinary Minister of Holy Communion at Church and Nursing Homes in the area. His engineering job brought him across the USA as well as Mexico, Europe and Asia where he enjoyed creating his own personal Pilgrimages to Holy Sites and sharing the experiences and pictures with family and friends. His retirement ambitions include enjoying his children and grandchildren, continued travel to holy sites around the world and sharing his Catholic faith wherever he can.